CUMBRIA LIBRARIES

3 8003 05206 5521

KT-151-679

THE KINGFISHER
DINOSAUR
ENCYCLOPEDIA

KINGFISHER

THE KINGFISHER
DINOSAUR
ENCYCLOPEDIA

KINGFISHER

First published 2009 by Kingfisher
This edition published 2021 by Kingfisher
an imprint of Macmillan Children's Books
The Smithson, 6 Briset Street, London EC1M 5NR
Associated companies throughout the world
www.panmacmillan.com

2021 edition:
Consultant Chris Barker
Senior editor Elizabeth Yeates
Designed by Intrepid Books

ISBN 978-0-7534-4641-6

Copyright © Macmillan Publishers International Ltd 2009, 2021

All rights reserved. No part of this publication may be reproduced, stored
in or introduced into a retrieval system, or transmitted, in any form or by any means
(electronic, mechanical, photocopying, recording or otherwise), without the prior written
permission of the publisher. Any person who does any unauthorized act in relation to this
publication may be liable to criminal prosecution and civil claims for damages.

3 5 7 9 8 6 4 2
2TR/1221/UTD/BBL/128MA

A CIP catalogue record for this book is available from the British Library.

Printed and bound by Bell and Bain Ltd. Glasgow

EU representative: 1st Floor, The Liffey Trust Centre,
117-126 Sheriff Street Upper, Dublin 1 D01 YC43

This book is sold subject to the condition that it shall not, by way
of trade or otherwise, be lent, resold, hired out, or otherwise circulated
without the publisher's prior consent in any form of binding or cover
other than that in which it is published and without a similar condition
including this condition being imposed on the subsequent purchaser.

Note to readers: the website addresses listed in this book are correct at the time of publishing.
However, due to the ever-changing nature of the Internet, website addresses and content can change.
Websites can contain links that are unsuitable for children. The publisher cannot be held responsible
for changes in website addresses or content, or for information obtained through third-party websites.
We strongly advise that Internet searches should be supervised by an adult.

MIX
Paper from
responsible sources
FSC® C116313

Contents

THE FIRST DINOSAURS

The first dinosaurs were small and rare. They scurried about on their hind legs, feeding on small prey such as reptiles. They lived in a world dominated by the distant relatives of modern crocodilians. However, a piece of luck at the end of the Triassic helped them to conquer the rest of the Mesozoic.

The prehistoric scene

Dinosaurs first evolved during the Triassic, about 240 million years ago. They were initially small and rare and lived alongside many other kinds of animals.

FROM LARGE TO SMALL
During the Middle Triassic, there were some amazing beasts living in Argentina.

Weighing up to 360kg, *Dinodontosaurus'* large size provided protection against many predators.

Massetognathus showed adaptations for a plant-based diet.

The crocodile-like *Chanaresuchus* may have been semi-aquatic, perhaps feeding on fish.

The tiny *Probelesodon* fed on insects and may have been preyed on by *Marasuchus*.

The rich collection of fossils discovered in the Chañares Formation in South America, revealed the diversity of some of these Triassic ecosystems.

Marasuchus

The first fossils of the pre-dinosaur *Marasuchus* were found in 235-million-year-old rocks. *Marasuchus* was tiny – only 40cm long – and had needle-sharp teeth. It was an active hunter that chased small, lizard-like animals.

Lagerpeton

Lagerpeton was about the size of a chicken, but much thinner. These little reptiles were close relatives of dinosaurs. They had long, slender legs and stood high on their toes, like a modern bird. Their legs were also tucked closely under their bodies.

Dinodontosaurus

This distant mammal-relative had a pair of tusk-like teeth, which may have been used for display and foraging. At the front of the snout was a horny beak that helped cut up the tough plants. *Dinodontosaurus* was large and round because its food was of poor quality, and it needed a huge gut in order to digest everything.

A strong skeleton

This skeleton of a *Dinodontosaurus* shows its massive arms and legs. They were heavily muscled to support a body that may have weighed a tonne or more. The limbs stick out at the sides a little, so *Dinodontosaurus* was probably not able to move very quickly.

Triassic palaeontology

Alfred Romer (1894–1973) was a great American palaeontologist (fossil expert) who discovered many of the remarkable Triassic beasts of South America. During expeditions in the 1950s, he and his team found up to 20 new species.

Massetognathus

This medium-sized cynodont was a distant relative to true mammals. It was a common animal based on the number of specimens found in comparison to other Chañares Formation fossils. Its skull measured up to 20cm in length.

Valley of dinosaurs

The Ischigualasto Valley in northern Argentina is key to an understanding of the very first dinosaurs. It is very hot and dry, but a fossil-hunter's paradise!

PALAEONTOLOGY IN ARGENTINA
Some of the most respected palaeontologists have worked in the Ischigualasto Valley.

Osavaldo Reig (1929–92) was the first to find dinosaurs in the valley.

José Bonaparte (1928–2020) worked with a team at Ischigualasto.

Paul Sereno (b.1957) found the most complete dinosaur fossils.

The first fossils were found in the 1950s. There have been many expeditions since then and remarkable fossils of the first dinosaurs have been unearthed.

Fossil finds

It takes many hours in the burning heat to dig out fossil bones. The bones are fragile and usually scattered, and the rock is hard. Palaeontologists have to chip away carefully, protecting the bones with glue and plaster so that they can be carried back to the laboratory.

On the surface

A collection of bones is laid out on a cloth before being individually packed up to go to a museum. Excavations have taken place in the valley since the 1920s, and over the years, many thousands of bones have been dug out. The area is now a World Heritage site.

The Ischigualasto Formation

The sandstones of the Ischigualasto Valley are called the Ischigualasto Formation. Some ash beds, just below the fossil layer, have enabled experts to date the rock sequence at 228 million years old. The ash beds were formed after a nearby volcano erupted.

AN EARLY HUNTER

HERRERASAURUS IS ONE OF THE EARLIEST KNOWN DINOSAURS FROM THE ISCHIGUALASTO FORMATION (LATE TRIASSIC) IN ARGENTINA. SEVERAL SKELETONS HAVE BEEN FOUND OF THIS 3–6M-LONG MEAT-EATER.

Between the eye socket and the nostril is a large opening, typical of many dinosaurs and their relatives. This likely housed a large air-filled cavity called a sinus, which probably helped *Herrerasaurus* control its body temperature.

Hunting dinosaurs simply tore up their food and swallowed it whole. The flesh of the prey was ground up in the stomach, and the bones were partly dissolved with stomach acids.

ACTIVE HUNTERS

Herrerasaurus was a fast-moving hunter. It fed on the small reptiles of Ischigualasto times, some of them about the size of lizards or rabbits. *Herrerasaurus* probably ran faster than its prey, using its slender skull and serrated teeth to capture its prey.

HIPS AND HINDLIMBS

Although *Herrerasaurus* was much larger than *Marasuchus*, and both animals look very similar, we know that *Herrerasaurus* was a dinosaur because of its hip bones. The hip socket for the thigh bone is open in *Herrerasaurus*, a 'new' trait common to dinosaurs. In *Marasuchus*, this hip socket had a bony inner wall instead, more like ancient reptiles.

Marasuchus, a close relative of the dinosaurs

Herrerasaurus, one of the first dinosaurs

INSIDE THE HEAD

The skull of *Herrerasaurus* has several openings. The pair of holes at the front of the snout are for the nostrils. At the very back are two openings, one above the other, for the jaw muscles. These muscles ran from the top of the skull down to the lower jaw and they gave *Herrerasaurus* a bite powerful enough to chop off a finger. In front is the round eye socket.

The Ischigualasto Formation

Many palaeontologists have searched these rocks in Argentina for fossils of dinosaurs and other animals.

Several Ischigualasto dinosaur skeletons, such as *Herrerasaurus* and *Eoraptor* have been found. Many other animals were living at this time too.

The 'dawn hunter'

Eoraptor means 'dawn hunter', and this small animal, about 1m long, ran quickly through the bushes and trees chasing small, lizard-sized prey. *Eoraptor* had multiple types of teeth in its jaws, suggesting a wide diet that might have included plants.

Eoraptor's head

This skull of *Eoraptor* is a beautiful fossil and it is nearly complete. Here, a fossil preparator is carefully removing the last pieces of rock from the ancient bones.

Eoraptor was about the size of an eight-year-old child.

Hyperodapedon

One of the most common reptiles in this area was *Hyperodapedon*, a rhynchosaur. The rhynchosaurs were plant-eaters that had massive jaws and great pavements of teeth for tearing up tough ferns and other plants. *Hyperodapedon* had a hooked snout, possibly for raking up plant roots and leaves.

Ischigualastia

The other major plant-eaters of the time were the dicynodonts, great hippo-sized animals that included *Ischigualastia* and *Dinodontosaurus* (see p.11). These large herbivores moved slowly through the bushes, pulling down leaves and fronds, too big to worry about attacks from dinosaurs.

Plant fossils

The rhynchosaurs and dicynodonts fed on ferns and seed ferns which were common in Ischigualasto times. Soon after, climates became drier, and these plants disappeared from much of the world.

Fossil *Dicroidium* (above) and the tree itself (right)

Pisanosaurus

Only a few bones of the plant-eater *Pisanosaurus* are known. Recent studies have placed it as a dinosaur relative or as an early type of ornithischian (see pp. 26–7).

HISTORICAL DATA

NAMING DINOSAURS

When the first dinosaurs were found, nobody knew what they were – some thought the bones came from giant lizards, others said they were crocodiles. Richard Owen (1804–92), examining various fossils in 1842, realized that they came from an extinct group. He invented the name 'dinosaur', which means 'fearfully great reptile'. Later, in 1881, he campaigned for the Natural History Museum (above) in London to be built to house natural specimens – including dinosaur fossils.

A changing world

The Late Triassic saw major changes in the types of animals living on land. Two extinction events provided new opportunities for the survivors.

The first mass extinction, called the Carnian Pluvial Episode (CPE), may have helped trigger the diversification of the dinosaurs, which until then had been rare components of Triassic ecosystems.

The Carnian Pluvial Episode

This extinction event occurred between 234–232 mya. Increased volcanic activity saw warming climates and substantial amounts of rainfall, which caused changes in the types of animals living on land. Common herbivores, such as dicynodonts (above), greatly suffered in this changing world. However, ancient cousins of crocodiles, as well as the first mammals, begin to appear, whilst dinosaurs began to take over as dominant land animals.

Plant evolution

The CPE saw changes in plant ecosystems, too. Several modern conifer and fern families begin to evolve. Lots of amber, or fossil tree sap, is known from this time, as wet conditions trigger more sap to be produced in modern conifers.

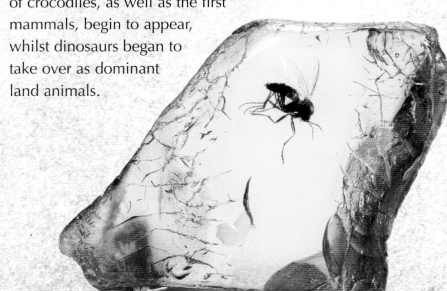

Tree resin fossilizes to form amber.

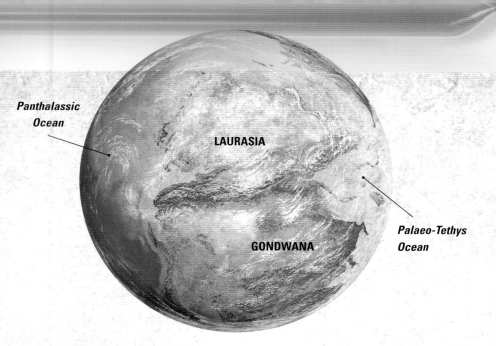

Panthalassic Ocean

LAURASIA

GONDWANA

Palaeo-Tethys Ocean

The world of the Carnian

During the Triassic, the continents formed a single supercontinent that stretched from the north pole to the south pole. This landmass came together as separate continents joined. It broke up slowly from the end of the Triassic.

The supercontinent was called Pangaea, and was made up of a southern continent, called Gondwana, and a northern continent, called Laurasia.

Footprint evidence

The diversification of dinosaurs can be seen in the types of footprints found in fossil sites. Before the CPE, footprints were exclusively made by a group of reptiles known as crurotarsans. When the CPE occurred, dinosaur tracks suddenly became more common. After the CPE, nearly all tracks can be attributed to dinosaurs, with crurotarsans' becoming rare.

Famous footprint sites in the alps show the change from crurotarsan to dinosaur-dominated faunas.

Plateosaurus

The first big dinosaurs, such as *Plateosaurus* from the Late Triassic of Germany, were plant-eaters. *Plateosaurus* could reach large sizes if food was in ample supply.

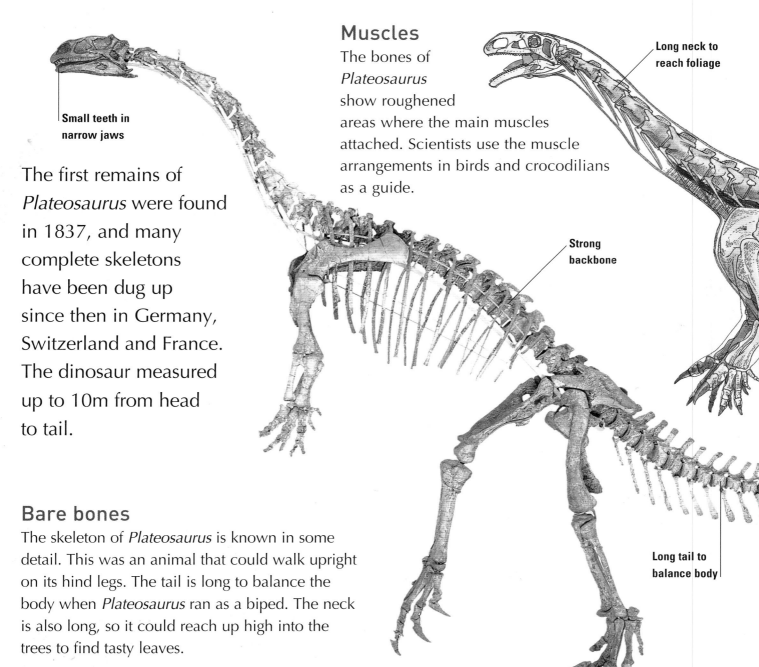

Small teeth in narrow jaws

Muscles

The bones of *Plateosaurus* show roughened areas where the main muscles attached. Scientists use the muscle arrangements in birds and crocodilians as a guide.

Long neck to reach foliage

The first remains of *Plateosaurus* were found in 1837, and many complete skeletons have been dug up since then in Germany, Switzerland and France. The dinosaur measured up to 10m from head to tail.

Strong backbone

Bare bones

The skeleton of *Plateosaurus* is known in some detail. This was an animal that could walk upright on its hind legs. The tail is long to balance the body when *Plateosaurus* ran as a biped. The neck is also long, so it could reach up high into the trees to find tasty leaves.

Long tail to balance body

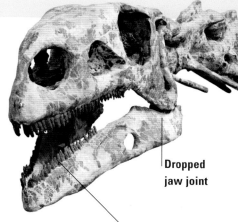

In the flesh

It is hard to add final details to a reconstruction of *Plateosaurus*. We do not know, for example, the colour of its skin. However, we do know the pattern of the skin. There are many fossils that show impressions of the scales in dinosaur skin.

Jaws and claws

Plateosaurus was one of the first plant-eating dinosaurs. Its jaws are narrow, and the jaw joint is dropped, giving a firm bite all along the jaw line. The teeth are small and not as sharp as flesh-eating dinosaurs. The hands, too, are modified for plant-eating. The long claws and strong fingers may have been used for gathering branches and pulling them towards the mouth.

Dropped jaw joint

Small, leaf-shaped teeth

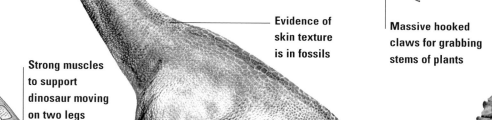

Skin colour uncertain

Lungs

Strong muscles to support dinosaur moving on two legs

Evidence of skin texture is in fossils

Massive hooked claws for grabbing stems of plants

A large gut helped to digest all of the plant matter eaten

The Trossingen bonebed

The most famous *Plateosaurus* find, at Trossingen, Germany, revealed the bodies of 50 or more individuals. Scientists puzzled for a long time about how they died.

Had they been trekking across a desert, and died from starvation and thirst? Or were they swept up in a sudden flash flood, and drowned? Modern studies of the rocks show their fossils were in mudstones from a floodplain.

First excavations

There were several major excavations at Trossingen. In the 1920s, Friedrich von Huene (1875–1969) directed huge teams of workmen, and half the hillside was dug away (above). The rock was carried away in small trucks (right) and the valuable bones taken to von Huene's university museum in nearby Tübingen.

Above: Friedrich von Huene

Right: Workers on the von Huene excavation

Modern excavation

New *Plateosaurus* remains are found from time to time. Most famous has been a huge dinosaur bone bed at Frick in Switzerland, discovered in 2007. A number of complete skeletons of *Plateosaurus* have been dug up, but it is estimated that there may be as many as another 100 skeletons to be found over the whole area.

How *Plateosaurus* moved

How did dinosaurs move? Palaeontologists can make computer models by scanning each bone, and coding the range of movements at each joint. *Plateosaurus* is now known to be a bipedal animal, moving on its hindlegs. Previous four-legged poses are inaccurate with the arms too short, which would have had limited movement.

Death in the mud

Many of the *Plateosaurus* specimens died upright, with their feet and legs found more deeply in the mudstone compared to the rest of their bodies. This strongly suggests these animals got stuck in the thick mudstone layer. This was deadly for the larger *Plateosaurus*, but the younger, smaller dinosaurs could break free. These animals appear to have died at different times, with some found higher up the floodplain than others.

Scientists map out *Plateosaurus'* joints to create a 3D computer model that shows how the dinosaur moved.

GHOST RANCH GRAVEYARD

ONE OF THE MOST SPECTACULAR DINOSAUR BONE BEDS WAS FOUND AT GHOST RANCH, NEW MEXICO, IN 1947. HUNDREDS OF SKELETONS OF THE SMALL FLESH-EATER *COELOPHYSIS* WERE DUG UP.

WHAT HAPPENED?

Studies revealed the mass grave was a result of many carcasses being transported by water and buried in the one site. It is not known what killed the animals. Maybe they died in a drought or were caught in a flood before their bones were washed away.

Coelophysis was a small hunter with excellent eyesight.

FOSSIL FINDS

Coelophysis makes up 95% of the fossil animals found at the quarry. Young and old *Coelophysis* can be distinguished. One famous specimen was thought to have been a cannibal with a baby *Coelophysis* in its stomach. A 2006 study showed the 'baby' was in fact a small reptile.

EDWIN COLBERT

Edwin H Colbert (1905–2001), shown in this photograph
(far right), was one of the most famous American dinosaur
palaeontologists. He began his career by studying fossil
mammals at the American Museum of Natural History in New
York City, USA. After excavating the Ghost Ranch site in 1947,
Colbert switched to studying dinosaurs and later wrote many
popular books about dinosaurs and continental drift.

DINOSAUR RELATIONSHIPS

THIS TRADTIONAL DINOSAUR TREE OF LIFE SHOWS US HOW GROUPS RELATE AND WHEN EACH GROUP CAME ON THE SCENE. AROUND 2000 SPECIES MAY HAVE EXISTED, BUT APPROXIMATELY HALF HAVE BEEN FOUND.

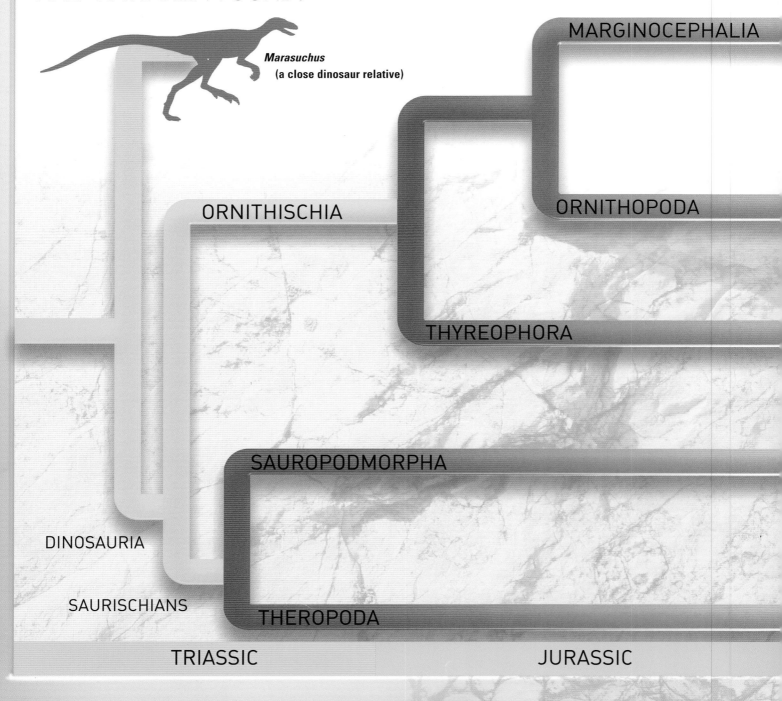

Marasuchus
(a close dinosaur relative)

MARGINOCEPHALIA

ORNITHISCHIA

ORNITHOPODA

THYREOPHORA

SAUROPODMORPHA

DINOSAURIA

SAURISCHIANS

THEROPODA

TRIASSIC

JURASSIC

Triceratops

Tenontosaurus

Stegosaurus

Argentinosaurus

Tyrannosaurus rex

CRETACIOUS

MAJOR GROUPS

Dinosaurs are usually split into two major groups based on their hip structure. Recently, a new tree has been proposed that suggests a completely different arrangement. Time will tell whether or not it is supported by future studies and new finds.

ORNITHISCHIAN PELVIC STRUCTURE

Despite meaning "bird-hipped", these dinosaurs were not related to birds, and none survived the end Cretaceous extinction event. The ornithischian hip had the pubis pointing backwards, which may have been driven by a different type of breathing pattern in this group.

SAURISCHIAN PELVIC STRUCTURE

Saurischian dinosaurs include the long-necked sauropodomorphs and the mainly carnivorous theropods (a group that includes modern birds). Most retained the ancestral hip bone orientations seen in other reptiles like lizards, with the pubis and ischium bones pointing in different directions.

The Bristol caves

Some amazing early fossils of the Late Triassic come from ancient caves in southwest England, UK.

BONES AND CAVES
The bones belonged to dinosaurs and ancestral lizards that lived on the limestone pavement.

Dinosaurs lived and died on the surface of the pavement.

Their carcasses were washed into the caves where they broke up.

The bones were buried in soil, to be uncovered millions of years later.

The animals lived on an upland limestone pavement that had been cracked by rainwater. Centuries of rain had created many cracks, ravines and caves in the limestone landscape.

Thecodontosaurus
The dinosaur found near Bristol is *Thecodontosaurus*, one of the first plant-eating dinosaurs. It was a small animal that walked on its hind legs, using its arms to gather plants. Its teeth were small and delicate, adapted for slicing plant stems and leaves.

The Bristol fauna
Side by side with the dinosaur *Thecodontosaurus* (top) lived a whole range of lizard-like animals, one of them called *Clevosaurus* (above). These are not true lizards, but relatives of the New Zealand tuatara (right), a small reptile that lives in burrows.

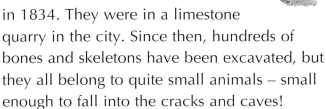

Kuehneosaurus **was about 70cm long, and its 'wings' were 14cm across.**

Kuehneosaurus

One of the most extraordinary Bristol creatures from the Late Triassic was a gliding animal. *Kuehneosaurus* had long ribs that stuck out at the side and were almost certainly covered with skin. It could leap and glide from tree to tree.

Fossil finds

The first fossils of the Bristol beasts – bones of *Thecodontosaurus* – were found in 1834. They were in a limestone quarry in the city. Since then, hundreds of bones and skeletons have been excavated, but they all belong to quite small animals – small enough to fall into the cracks and caves!

Revealed in the rocks

As the quarrymen work through the great walls of limestone, they sometimes spot a reddish streak (right). The red rock is sand or mud filling an ancient cave system. This contains plants and – rarely – insects. Quite often there are the bones of small creatures – *Clevosaurus* and its relatives, and the gliding *Kuehneosaurus*. Palaeontologists have to sieve the sediment and pick out the delicate bones very carefully, sometimes using a dental drill.

Dinosaurs take over

Dinosaur numbers increased following two extinction events in the Triassic. Dinosaurs weren't the dominant land animals during much of the Triassic, so the disappearance of their competitors at the end of the Triassic, meant the dinosaurs were free to diversify.

The end-Triassic mass extinction

This happened 201 million years ago, and it did not just affect reptiles and dinosaurs on land. It was also a time when many groups of shellfish and fishes in the sea, as well as land plants and other animals, disappeared. Explanations have included the impact of a giant asteroid and global warming.

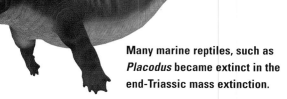

Many marine reptiles, such as *Placodus* became extinct in the end-Triassic mass extinction.

Survivors

The successful archosaur group known as the Pseudosuchia dominated for much of the Triassic, keeping dinosaurs in check. But only one group – the crocodylomorphs (such as Protosuchus, above) – made it through into the Jurassic. Quite when other pseudosuchian groups became extinct is unclear, as some may have died out before the Triassic-Jurassic extinction event.

Pterosurs, such as *Eudimorphodon* flourished throughout the Mesozic.

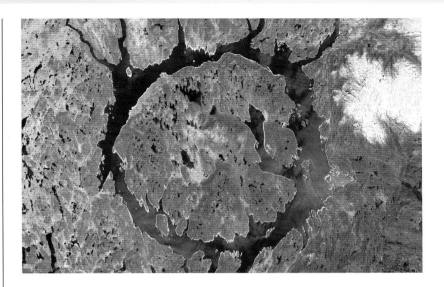

A new boundary

The boundary between the Triassic and Jurassic can be seen in many parts of the world. In Europe, this was a time of change, when red rocks were deposited in hot deserts, and lakes and rivers gave way to marine rocks. There was a great flooding of the sea over Europe, and in places the switch from red desert rocks to black marine rocks is clear.

The Manicouagan crater

There was great excitement in the 1980s when a huge crater, about 100km wide, was identified in Canada. It was only when scientists saw the first satellite photographs that they could see the very clear circular outline, now filled with rivers and lakes. The crater was first dated at the Triassic–Jurassic boundary, but we now know that it is much older, at 215 million years.

Global warming

There were major volcanic eruptions on the site of the North Atlantic as the great ocean began to open up. These rifts were driven by volcanic eruptions that sent clouds of gas into the atmosphere. There was a time of global warming and many scientists think this was a key driver of the mass extinction.

Dinosaur facts

The Triassic Period followed and ended with a mass extinction, when half or more of the species on Earth disappeared. The end of the non-bird dinosaurs, 66 mya, was another mass extinction. These were three of five such crises for life on Earth.

THE FIVE GREAT EXTINCTIONS

This diagram (right) shows the way life has expanded through time. The first life in the sea arose 3,500 mya, deep in the Precambrian era. Then sea creatures became more common and larger at the beginning of the Palaeozoic era, 540 mya. Plants and insects moved onto land about 450 mya, followed by the first amphibians 400 mya. The first two mass extinctions had major effects on life in the sea. Then, at the end of the Palaeozoic came the biggest crisis of all. The fourth and fifth mass extinctions ended the Triassic (see pp.30–1) and the Cretaceous (see pp.150–1).

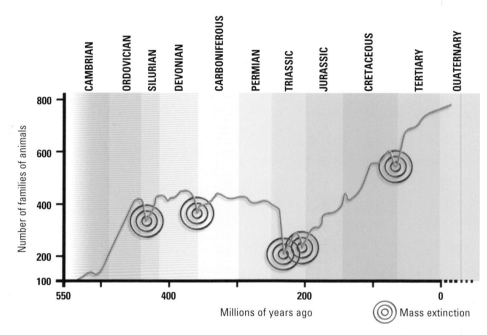

A *Coelophysis* fossil, with its last meal – a crocodile ancestor – in its stomach, found at Ghost Ranch in 1947

WEBSITES ON GEOLOGICAL TIME AND MASS EXTINCTIONS

www.ucmp.berkeley.edu/exhibits/index.php   A guide to the history of life.

www.cotf.edu/ete/modules/msese/earthsysflr/geotime.html   Work your way through time.

www.fossilmuseum.net/GeologicalTimeMachine.htm   The geological timescale.

www.pbs.org/wgbh/nova/evolution/brief-history-life.html   The history of life on Earth.

DINOSAURS DIVERSIFY

With most of their competitors lost during the end Triassic mass extinction, dinosaurs were able to explore new lifestyles and diversified during the Jurassic. New groups, like the armoured dinosaurs, make an appearance, whilst birds take to the skies for the first time.

Dinosaurs of South Africa

A mass extinction at the end of the Triassic displaced many of the dinosaur's main competitors. The Jurassic saw previously rare groups, such as the ornithischians, increase in numbers.

Ornithischians – bird-hipped dinosaurs – are known from the Elliott Formation and the Clarens Formation of South Africa. These formations are famous for their wealth of post-Triassic life and continue to produce remarkable finds.

Lesothosaurus

Lesothosaurus was one of the smaller Elliot Formation dinosaurs. Perhaps an early ornithischian, the tooth wear patterns on its teeth do not match the semi-arid plants of the time. It's been suggested an omnivorous diet may have helped this dinosaur survive the seasonal climates, when food was sometimes hard to find.

Many ornithischians had a small bone called the palpebral that pointed into the eye socket. Connective tissue was attached to help support the eyeball.

Palpebral

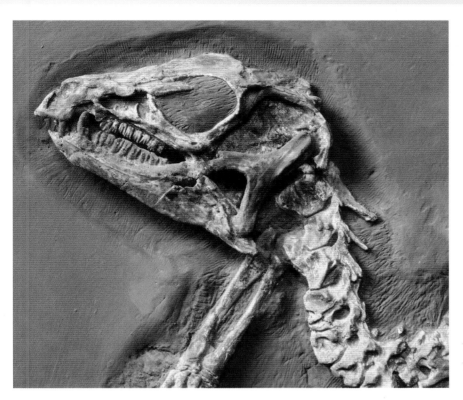

Heterodontosaurus

Heterodontosaurus had a peculiar set of differently shaped teeth lining its jaws. This differs from most reptiles who usually have similar shaped teeth throughout the jaw. Two pairs of fang-like 'canines' may have helped to snip off tough vegetation, whilst the teeth at the back helped to break it down.

The lower fang was so huge there is a deep pit in the side of the snout for it.

Massospondylus

This giant plant-eating dinosaur was a relative of *Plateosaurus* (see pp.20–1). At 4m long, it may have weighed up to a tonne. Eggs and extremely rare nearly hatched individuals have been discovered for this dinosaur.

The long neck was useful for reaching high into trees.

The tiny teeth were used for cutting leaves but not for chewing.

The Kayenta Formation

In Arizona, in the southwestern USA, there is an area famous for fossils of Early Jurassic dinosaurs.

The rocks were laid down in hot, dry conditions. They preserved hundreds of skeletons of dinosaurs, crocodiles, mammals and other creatures.

The Kayenta outcrop

The Kayenta Formation is over 100m thick in some places, and it is made up of layers of red, orange and yellow sandstones and mudstones. The red colours are mainly due to iron reacting with oxygen, giving the rock a rust-like appearance.

Sand dune features

The Kayenta sandstones were mainly laid down by rivers flowing across an arid environment and around sand dunes nearly 200 million years ago. These rivers flowed west and some occasionally dried out completely. Life must have been tough for the animals and plants of the region.

The badlands

Today, the Kayenta Formation is located in a large desert in northern Arizona. In the modern Arizona desert, the rocks often stand up as wild bluffs and pinnacles, a backdrop to many cowboy films! Modern winds have shaped the rocks. Rare torrential rain swells the streams in the ravines, and these hurtle across the countryside, cutting great gashes, and removing soil and plants. Normally, only cactuses and sagebrush can grow in such dry conditions.

Kayenta dinosaurs

Dinosaurs from the Kayenta include large meat-eaters and early relatives of armoured dinosaurs.

The Early Jurassic rocks are filled with other animals, including fish, amphibians and small mammal relatives.

Footprint
Identifying the track-makers of the many footprints found in the Kayenta Formation is tricky, however some were likely made by *Dilophosaurus* or its close cousins.

Coelophysis
Coelophysis was a small flesh-eating dinosaur. Whilst some *Coelophysis* species lived in the Triassic, the one in the Kayenta sandstones was a close Early Jurassic cousin, and had two small ridges on its snout.

Dilophosaurus had long slender teeth and a relatively weak bite

Dilophosaurus
The most amazing dinosaur from the Kayenta Formation is *Dilophosaurus*, excavated in the 1940s, and first identified as *Megalosaurus*, a dinosaur already known from the Middle Jurassic of England (see pp.56–7). Most striking of all were the head crests – two thin bone ridges that run the length of the skull. Their function is uncertain. They were probably used for signalling 'Look out!' or 'I'm looking for a mate' to other *Dilophosaurus*.

Protosuchus skeleton

Protosuchus was a small relative of modern crocodilians, whose bones are known from the Early Jurassic Moenave Formation of Arizona. The skull was short and wide at the back, creating more space for the jaw closing muscles. Its eyes faced forwards a little, helping it judge distances better, and it probably hunted prey on land.

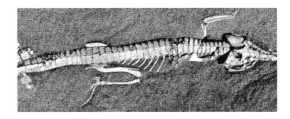

Protosuchus

Protosuchus was only 1m long, but was covered with bony plates down its back. These plates may have helped support the body as it moved on land.

Camp and Welles

Many of the Kayenta beasts were collected and studied by two great palaeontologists from the University of California at Berkeley, Charles Camp (1893–1975) and Sam Welles (1909–97). Camp worked on many different fossil groups, from lizards to dinosaurs, and taught Sam Welles.

CULTURAL NOTE

DINOSAURS IN THE MOVIES

Dinosaurs have appeared in movies for nearly 100 years. *Dilophosaurus* was a star of the popular 1993 film *Jurassic Park*, directed by Steven Spielberg. The film is famous as the for its computer-generated images were used to good effect. In the film, *Dilophosaurus* is inaccurately shown as being one-quarter of its real size, had a crest round its neck that could be expanded as a warning, and could spit poison at its attackers!

Dinosaur footprints

The Kayenta Formation is one of the places famous for dinosaur footprints as well as skeletons. The footprints tell us a great deal about how dinosaurs lived.

A track of prints tells us about the behaviour of a particular dinosaur – any potential injuries or the speed it was moving, for example.

MAKING FOOTPRINTS

Dinosaur footprints give clues about the animal that made them. These fossils provide invaluable information for palaeontologists.

The dinosaur steps on soft mud and sand, leaving an impression.

The footprint impression fills up with more sand or mud.

Over a period of millions of years, the mud gradually turns to rock.

The material filling the impression washes out, leaving a rocky footprint.

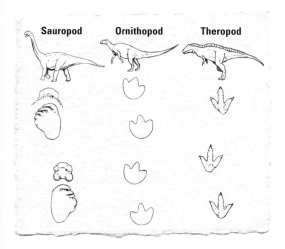

Sauropod   Ornithopod   Theropod

Track types

Dinosaur footprints can be identified to major groups at least. They vary enormously in size from little prints the size of a 50 pence coin, to massive prints nearly 2 metres across made by sauropods. Some prints can even preserve imprints of the scales and fatty pads under the foot.

Calculating speed

If an animal walks, its footprints are close together. If it runs fast, they are far apart. Scientists can use equations based on modern animals to deduce an approximate size and running speed of a dinosaur based on its tracks.

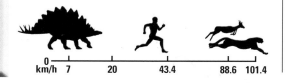

0 km/h   7   20   43.4   88.6 101.4

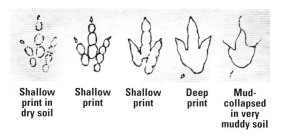

Shallow print in dry soil   Shallow print   Shallow print   Deep print   Mud-collapsed in very muddy soil

Interpreting tracks

Tracks show many other things apart from what made the prints and how fast they were moving. Some tracks show animals moving together in groups and there's one track that appears to show a predator tracking its prey.

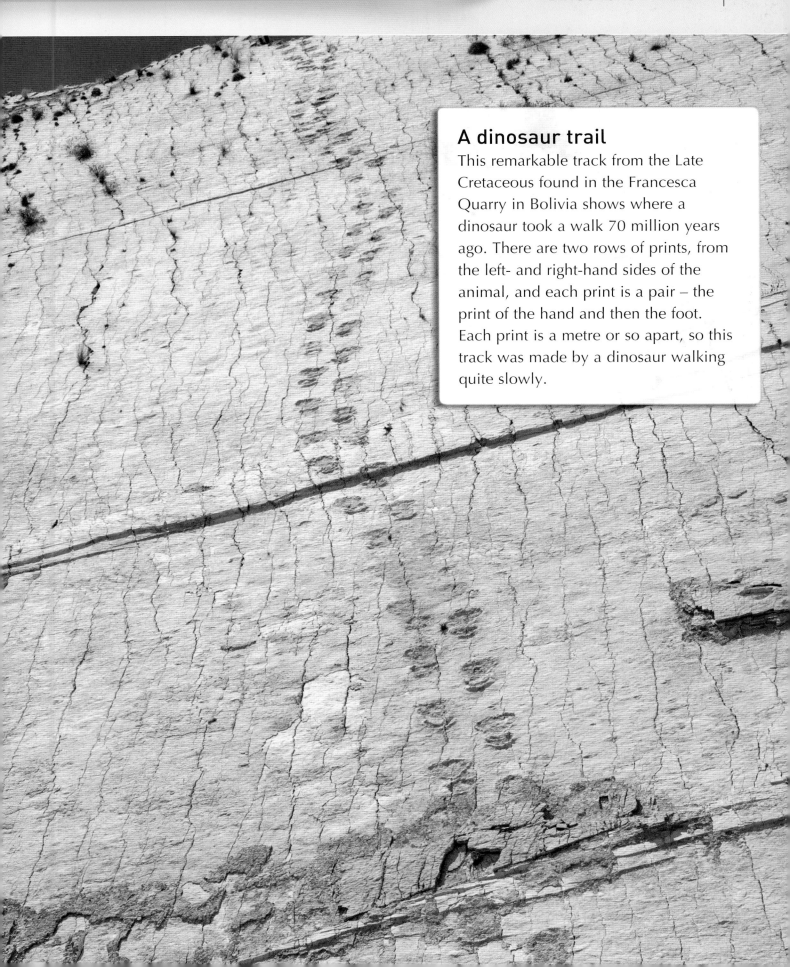

A dinosaur trail

This remarkable track from the Late Cretaceous found in the Francesca Quarry in Bolivia shows where a dinosaur took a walk 70 million years ago. There are two rows of prints, from the left- and right-hand sides of the animal, and each print is a pair – the print of the hand and then the foot. Each print is a metre or so apart, so this track was made by a dinosaur walking quite slowly.

Dinosaurs of Lufeng

China is famous for its dinosaurs, and some of the first to be discovered in that country were the Lufeng dinosaurs, unearthed in the 1930s.

The Lufeng Formation is Early Jurassic in age, similar to the Kayenta Formation. Sauropodomorphs are common finds here, sharing habitats with several theropods and even early mammal relatives.

Lufengosaurus

Lufengosaurus was a common dinosaur in the China region, and it probably walked on its hindlimbs in search of plants. Large hands and powerful arms may have played a role in foraging or possibly fighting. Scientists have even discovered embryos of this dinosaur, and have shown they moved inside their eggs like modern birds.

Tiny head

Long neck

Yunnanosaurus

Fossils of *Yunnanosaurus*, a relative of *Lufengosaurus*, are much less common. It had unusual spoon-shaped teeth that are similar to some later sauropod dinosaurs (see pp.60–1).

Long tail

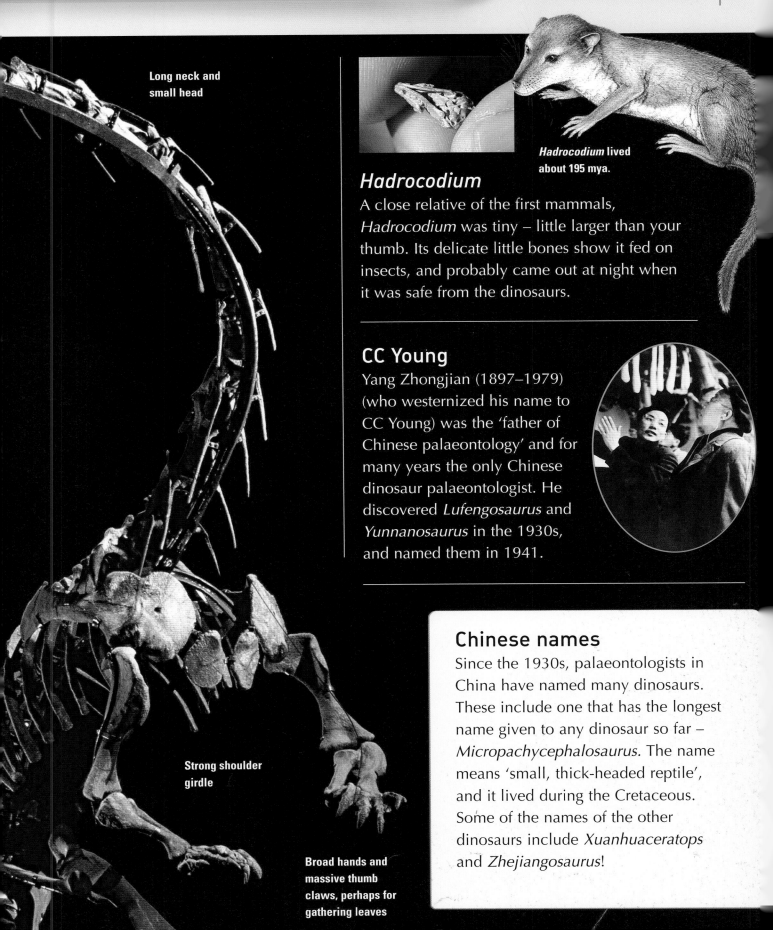

Long neck and
small head

Hadrocodium lived
about 195 mya.

Hadrocodium

A close relative of the first mammals,
Hadrocodium was tiny – little larger than your
thumb. Its delicate little bones show it fed on
insects, and probably came out at night when
it was safe from the dinosaurs.

CC Young

Yang Zhongjian (1897–1979)
(who westernized his name to
CC Young) was the 'father of
Chinese palaeontology' and for
many years the only Chinese
dinosaur palaeontologist. He
discovered *Lufengosaurus* and
Yunnanosaurus in the 1930s,
and named them in 1941.

Strong shoulder
girdle

Broad hands and
massive thumb
claws, perhaps for
gathering leaves

Chinese names

Since the 1930s, palaeontologists in
China have named many dinosaurs.
These include one that has the longest
name given to any dinosaur so far –
Micropachycephalosaurus. The name
means 'small, thick-headed reptile',
and it lived during the Cretaceous.
Some of the names of the other
dinosaurs include *Xuanhuaceratops*
and *Zhejiangosaurus*!

ARMOURED DINOSAURS

THE EARLIEST FOSSIL EVIDENCE OF ARMOURED DINOSAURS, ALSO KNOWN AS THYREOPHORANS, COMES FROM THE EARLY JURASSIC. OSTEODERMS (BONES) GREW IN THE SKIN AND PROVIDED SOME PROTECTION AGAINST PREDATORS.

THE FIRST SKELETON

Scelidosaurus was one of the first known thyreophorans, with a complex array of osteoderms projecting from its body. Material belonging to *Scelidosaurus* was initially discovered during the late 19th Century on the south coast of England, during a time when dinosaurs were only known from teeth and other material. The discovery of a skeleton was an important find, as it was the first known skeleton of any dinosaur.

DYNAMICS OF A FOSSIL

This fossil shows the skull and neck of a *Scelidosaurus*, with large armour plates running down the back of the neck. Part of the tip of the snout was broken off when the fossil was collected. *Scelidosaurus'* small, leaf-shaped teeth, good for chopping ferns, are clearly visible along each jaw.

SKIN FOSSILS

This section of the skin of a *Scelidosaurus* (below) shows many small bone plates in a crazy-paving pattern, just as they would have been in life. Skeletons of *Scelidosaurus* were sometimes washed into the sea, and the flesh and skin lost. This one must have been buried deep in the mud before any sharks or crabs could tear off its skin and flesh.

Different-sized plates (scutes) ran along the back, neck and tail of *Scelidosaurus*.

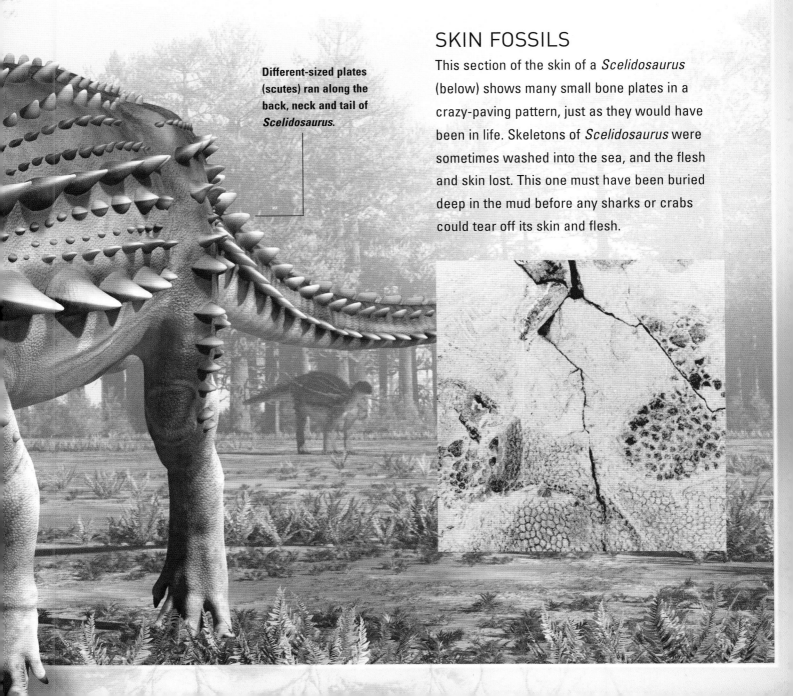

The geological record

How do we know the ages of all the dinosaurs, and date the rocks in which they are found? We find out this information from stratigraphy.

Stratigraphy is the study of strata, or rock layers. Early scientists thought rocks and fossils were found randomly in different places, without any real meaning. Then, the first geologists – experts on rocks – realized that there were patterns.

	ERA	PERIOD	EVENTS
0	Cenozoic	Quaternary	Evolution of humans
2 mya		Neogene	Mammals diversify
66 mya		Palaeogene	
100 mya	Mesozoic	Cretaceous	Extinction of non-bird dinosaurs First flowering plants
145 mya			
		Jurassic	First birds Dinosaurs diversify
201 mya			
		Triassic	Possible first mammals First dinosaurs
251 mya			
	Palaeozoic	Permian	Major extinction
298 mya			
		Carboniferous	First reptiles Lush forest habitats
358 mya			
		Devonian	First tetrapods Jawed fish diversify
419 mya			
443 mya		Silurian	First vascular land plants
		Ordovician	Possible appearance of first jawed fish
485 mya			
		Cambrian	Diversification of complex life First chordates
541 mya			
	Neoproterozoic	Precambrian	First soft-bodied metazoans First animal traces
1000 mya			

A geological time scale

Younger rocks lie on top of older rocks. So, by working up and down cliffs and quarries, geologists can work out the relative ages of the rocks, from most ancient to most recent. In the 1820s and 1830s, experts began to divide up the great thicknesses of rocks into geological periods – Triassic, Jurassic, Cretaceous. Later, they were able to calculate exact dates, in millions of years, using the rate of decay of radioactive minerals.

Index fossils

Certain animals, such as ammonites, evolve quickly into new species and only live for short spans of geological time. As a result, these 'index fossils' only usually appear in specific strata. This is useful for dating unknown rocks, as you can match their fossils to previously dated strata containing the same fossils.

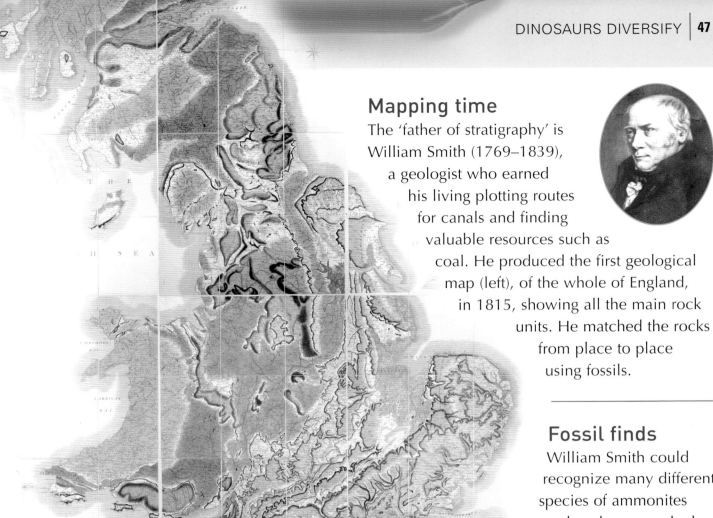

Mapping time

The 'father of stratigraphy' is William Smith (1769–1839), a geologist who earned his living plotting routes for canals and finding valuable resources such as coal. He produced the first geological map (left), of the whole of England, in 1815, showing all the main rock units. He matched the rocks from place to place using fossils.

Fossil finds

William Smith could recognize many different species of ammonites and each one marked a particular age zone in the rocks. Ammonites swam in the Mesozoic seas, with bodies like squid or octopus inside a circular shell.

Fossil ammonites

The cliffs of Lyme Regis

Some of the most famous Lias fossils, including the armoured dinosaur *Scelidosaurus*, come from cliffs near the small fishing town of Lyme Regis in Dorset, southern England. The layers of limestone and mudstone were quarried for building stone. The ammonites and other fossil shellfish, as well as occasional bones, are collected by many people.

MARINE GIANTS

WHILST DINOSAURS WALKED ON LAND, MARINE REPTILES OF ALL SHAPES AND SIZES STALKED THE JURASSIC SEAS. THEY FED ON AMMONITES, FISH... AND EACH OTHER!

DANGEROUS WATERS

Ichthyosaurs, or 'fish lizards', were some of the common marine reptiles to patrol the Jurassic seas. Ichthyosaurs looked like modern sharks or dolphins. They swam fast by beating their tail from side to side, and fed on a range of seafood, like ammonite to other marine reptiles, depending on the species. Another group of reptile, the plesiosaurs, swam by 'underwater flying', beating their paddles and pursuing fish and even smaller ichthyosaurs.

A coiled ammonite

The plesiosaur *Pliosaurus*

The ichthyosaur
Ichthyosaurus

MARY ANNING

Mary Anning (1799–1847) is one of the most famous fossil collectors. She found ichthyosaur and plesiosaur fossils at Lyme Regis, as well as flying reptiles fossils and many ammonites and fishes. She had a keen insight on the biology of these extinct animals, but was often overlooked by the male scientists of the time.

FOSSIL FINDS

Some of the fossils found in the Lyme Regis area are amazing. This near complete ichthyosaur fossil shows the long-pointed snout and the front paddles below the rib cage. The body must have fallen to the sea bed and been covered by black mud without undergoing any disturbance.

Dinosaurs of Antarctica

The first dinosaurs from Antarctica were found only 30 years ago, and several skeletons have been excavated since. The effort needed to dig the fossils out of the icy ground is

In the Mesozoic, Antarctica was not covered with ice, climates were warmer and there were lush forests.

Working in Antarctica

Expeditions cost a great deal of money. Ships, planes and helicopters are needed to carry people and equipment to the site. The continent is a protected site and human interferance must be minimal and so absolutely everything has to be brought home. Even the scientists' urine and other waste has to be taken away.

In the field

During the southern summer in Antarctica, the snow melts and geologists can see the rocks. During this short summer season, the scientists must complete their work as fast as they can. Even though the snow has melted, the air is still cold, and they have to wear thick clothes.

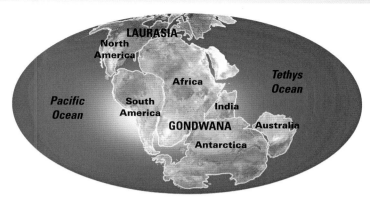

Connected continents

Today, Antarctica is a huge island that lies over the south pole. During the Mesozoic, Antarctica was connected to several other continents. Although the winters were cool, and some places saw no sun for several months, many dinosaurs appear to have stayed in the region.

Glacialisaurus

'Frozen reptile' is a good name for an Antarctic dinosaur, but this Early Jurassic animal did not live on the ice. It is known from only a few leg bones found on Mount Kirkpatrick, but these show that it was a "prosauropod" related to *Lufengosaurus* from China (see pp.42–3).

Cryolophosaurus

The first Antarctic dinosaur to be named was also the most spectacular. *Cryolophosaurus* was a theropod with an extraordinary bony crest on its forehead, just in front of the eyes. The crest may have been brightly coloured and used for signalling.

Tritylodontids

Other fossils from the Early Jurassic of Antarctica include fragments of a pterosaur and some other dinosaurs, as well as tree trunks and other plants. One unusual fossil is a tritylodontid (below), known from a single tooth. Tritylodontids were close relatives of mammals and they fed on tough plants that they ground up with massive teeth.

THE ORIGIN OF BIRDS

PEOPLE OFTEN SAY
THAT BIRDS ARE 'LIVING
DINOSAURS', BUT WHAT
DOES THIS MEAN? CAREFUL
STUDY OF DINOSAUR BONES
ALLOWS SCIENTISTS TO
DRAW DETAILED FAMILY TREES.
IT IS CLEAR FROM THESE
THAT BIRDS ARE DINOSAURS.

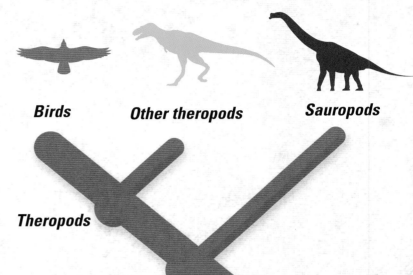

Birds **Other theropods** **Sauropods**

Theropods

**Saurischians
(lizard-hipped
dinosaurs)**

Special dyes help reveal bone growth in bird embryos.

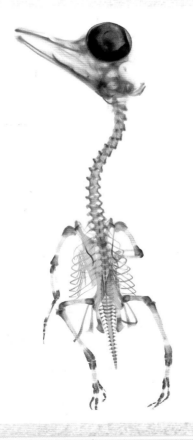

EMBRYO SECRETS

Birds are highly specialized animals, and many of the ancestral theropod features have been lost or modified. But thanks to modern science, it is now possible to find evidence of lost bones in the embryos of living birds. A well-known dinosaur skull bone like the postorbital, which forms the back of the eye socket, was thought to be absent in birds. By looking at avian embryos, the postorbital is actually present, but it fuses to the rest of the skull early on in bird development. This explains why palaeontologists used to think it was absent altogether.

ANCESTRAL LINE

Birds share many characteristics with theropod dinosaurs, ranging from specialised wrist bones, a hollow skeleton and feathers. The first bird, *Archaeopteryx*, shows many of the features seen in its ancestors, such as clawed hands and a long bony tail.

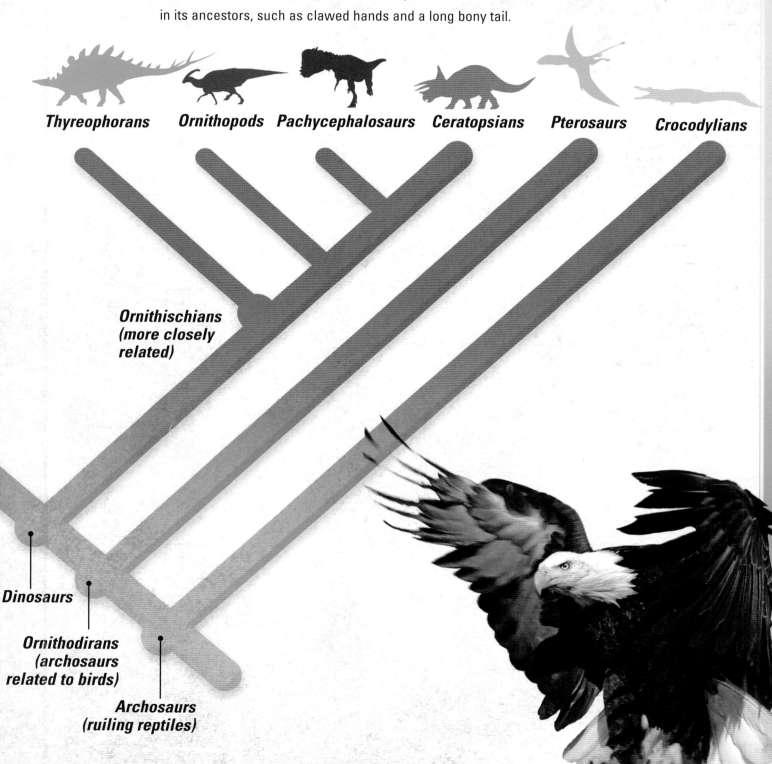

Thyreophorans   **Ornithopods**   **Pachycephalosaurs**   **Ceratopsians**   **Pterosaurs**   **Crocodylians**

*Ornithischians
(more closely
related)*

Dinosaurs

*Ornithodirans
(archosaurs
related to birds)*

*Archosaurs
(ruiling reptiles)*

Theropods

Many theropods were meat-eaters, but several groups evolved toothless beaks, becoming herbivorous.

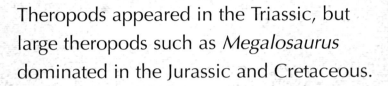

THEROPOD SKULLS
Theropod habits show in their skulls, which differ in snout length, tooth shape and jaw power.

Tyrannosaurus' skull was wide at the back to allow for huge bone-crushing muscles.

Allosaurus had strong skull, helping it deal with the stresses of catching prey.

Spinosaurs such as *Suchomimus* had long, crocodile-like snouts, adapted for eating fish.

Carcharodontosaurus' jaws and 'steak-knife' teeth could have held a 512kg object.

Theropods appeared in the Triassic, but large theropods such as *Megalosaurus* dominated in the Jurassic and Cretaceous.

Teeth

The basic theropod tooth was curved backwards with serrated edges, which helped slice through muscle. However, theropods experimented with their diets throughout their evolution, and a great variety of tooth shapes appeared during the Mesozoic.

Bipedal stance

Theropods all ran on their hind legs, and kept their arms free. If prey was small enough, it was swallowed whole. However, bigger carcasses needed to be pinned down by the foot whilst the skull and neck helped tear manageable chunks off.

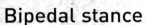

The wrong shape

The first theropod to be found, *Megalosaurus* (see pp.56–7), was known first only from a few bones. Its discoverer, William Buckland, thought it was a giant lizard. The drawing (above) shows something that is a cross between a lion and a crocodile!

Cretaceous food web

When many fossils are found in the same deposit, it may be possible to work out the food web – the pattern of who ate what. In the Cretaceous, the main plant-eaters were dinosaurs, and they were eaten by theropod dinosaurs. On the ground, smaller animals such as mammals were also part of the food web, but they probably fed on insects, and were eaten in turn by small predators such as crocodiles, or even by theropods.

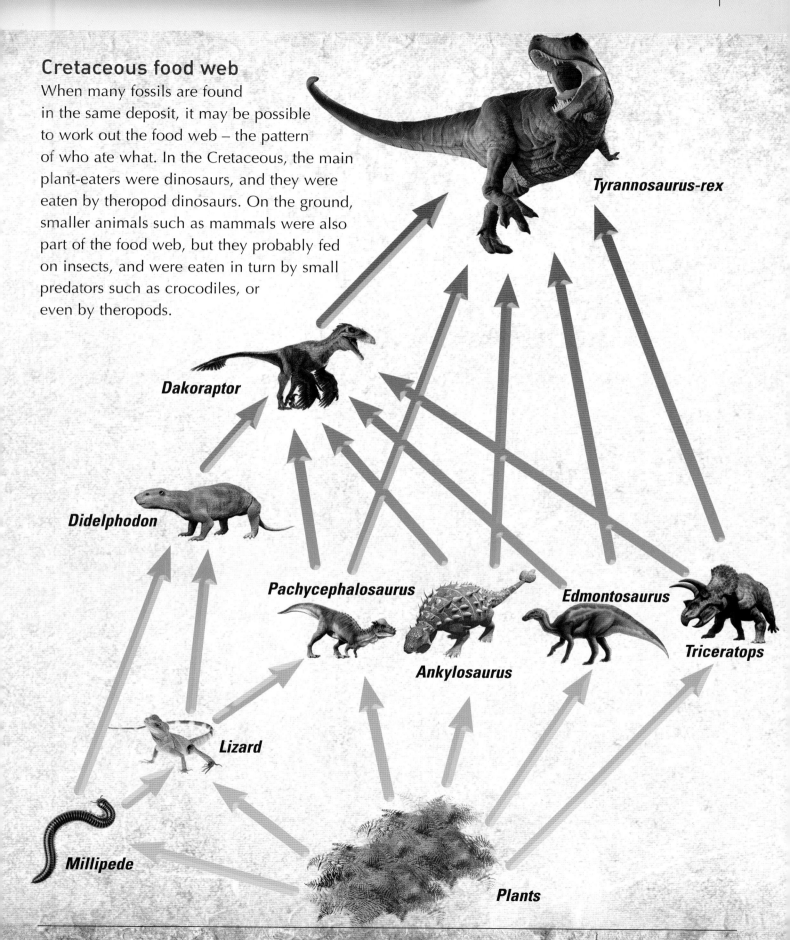

Tyrannosaurus-rex

Dakoraptor

Didelphodon

Pachycephalosaurus

Ankylosaurus

Edmontosaurus

Triceratops

Lizard

Millipede

Plants

The tail of a theropod such as *Megalosaurus* was extremely muscular. This allowed it to keep its balance as it ran on its two hind legs. The bottom of the tail anchored a large muscle that joined onto the back of the leg, helping pull the leg back with force as it moved.

MEGALOSAURUS

THE TERROR OF THE MIDDLE JURASSIC, *MEGALOSAURUS* WAS 6M LONG AND WEIGHED UP TO A TONNE. THIS THEROPOD WALKED ON ITS HIND LEGS WITH A LONG TAIL COUNTER BALANCING THE BODY. IT WAS LIKELY THE LARGEST LAND PREDATOR OF ITS TIME AND PROWLED THE ANCIENT FORESTS OF EUROPE.

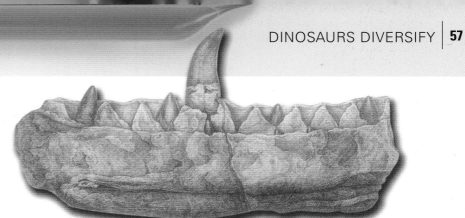

Buckland's drawing of the right lower jaw bone of *Megalosaurus*

FIERCE PREDATOR

Despite being one of the first dinosaurs ever formally described, *Megalosaurus* is known from a few bones and no complete skeleton has yet been found. Palaeontologists have to compare the remains to other, better known theropods to estimate its size and habits.

NAMING A DINOSAUR

In 1824, *Megalosaurus* became the first dinosaur to be named anywhere in the world. William Buckland (1784–1856) did not collect the fossils himself. They were found by collectors near Oxford, England. The name means 'big lizard', and at the time dinosaurs didn't formally exist in science – the term dinosaur would only first appear almost 20 years later.

Anatomy of defence

The stegosaurs flourished in the Middle and Late Jurassic. They had remarkable spines and sets of plates, which are likely to have had multiple roles in a stegosaur's life.

The plates and spikes of stegosaurs were made out of bones that grew directly in the skin, called osteoderms. In many stegosaurs, these not only lined the back and tail, but also the shoulders.

The hand bones of many stegosaurs were arranged in a semi circle to help support their bulk. A similar arrangement was also found in the sauropods.

Dacentrurus

One of the biggest stegosaurs, *Dacentrurus* is best known from the Late Jurassic of Portugal, France and England. However, there are no complete skeletons. It may have been 6–10m long, and had two rows of small plates and spines down the middle of its back.

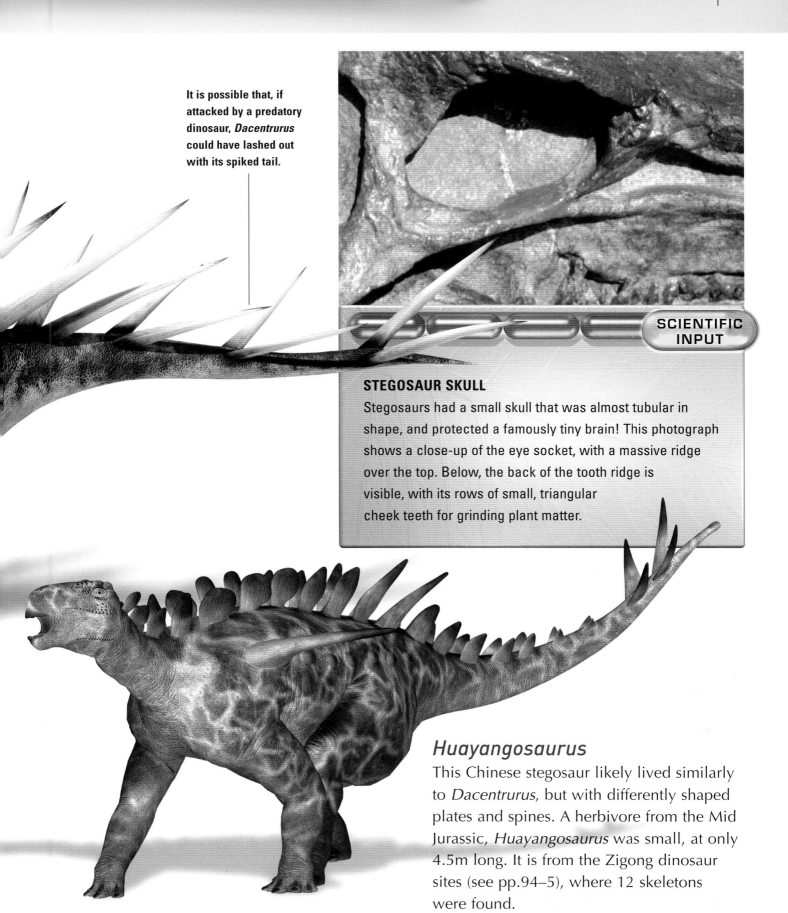

It is possible that, if attacked by a predatory dinosaur, *Dacentrurus* could have lashed out with its spiked tail.

SCIENTIFIC INPUT

STEGOSAUR SKULL
Stegosaurs had a small skull that was almost tubular in shape, and protected a famously tiny brain! This photograph shows a close-up of the eye socket, with a massive ridge over the top. Below, the back of the tooth ridge is visible, with its rows of small, triangular cheek teeth for grinding plant matter.

Huayangosaurus

This Chinese stegosaur likely lived similarly to *Dacentrurus*, but with differently shaped plates and spines. A herbivore from the Mid Jurassic, *Huayangosaurus* was small, at only 4.5m long. It is from the Zigong dinosaur sites (see pp.94–5), where 12 skeletons were found.

SAUROPODS

The Mesozoic saw some of the largest animals to ever walk the earth: the sauropods. Whilst some of their 'prosauropod' cousins, *Plateosaurus*, walked on two legs, the giant size of the sauropods meant they had to move around on all fours. Their extreme sizes have fascinated palaeontologists, and many species are well studied as a result.

GIANTS ON EARTH

The early sauropods, such as *Shunosaurus* and *Cetiosaurus* from the Middle Jurassic, were medium-sized sauropods. Later sauropods such as *Argentinosaurus* may have weighed up to 80 tonnes. Baby sauropods were only 5kg or so when they hatched, and some species took decades to grow to full adult size.

DIET OF PLANTS

To fuel their massive bulks, sauropods had to eat a lot of plants. It's been estimated that a 10 tonne *Diplodocus* would possibly needed to eat 33kg of ferns a day, whilst an 80 tonne *Argentinosaurus* may have gulped down over 200kg of plants per day!

Cycad

Tree fern

Horsetails

ON THE MOVE...

Different types of sauropods appear to show different social groups. The footprints of some species indicate they moved around in groups of similar-aged individuals based on the size of the tracks. However, at other localities, both younger and older individuals moved together.

In the laboratory

When it comes to finding clues about life in the past, tiny fossils can be as useful as giant bones.

Fossil hunters have to wash and sieve tonnes of sediment in the laboratory in order to separate out the teeth and bones of tiny creatures.

Hornsleasow

The Middle Jurassic of central England, UK, has produced amazing evidence of the smaller animals of the day. One site at Hornsleasow has proved especially rich. Ten tonnes of sand have preserved thousands of bones of fishes, frogs, salamanders, crocodilians and turtles that lived in small ponds, as well as plant remains.

The pointed tooth of the plant-eating *Stereognathus*, a small relative of modern mammals.

Hornsleasow fossils

The Hornsleasow fossils include crocodilians and small theropod dinosaurs that hunted early lizards and small mammals. The mammal fossils are very rare, but a few species have been identified that lived by feeding on insects. There are also a few bones of flying pterosaurs.

An artist's impression of the world of the animals of Hornsleasow.

Sieving

Small fossils can be found by careful searching in the field, but sieving is better. Bags of sediment are washed to remove mud, and then carefully sieved. Small pieces of sediment pass through the sieve, and the bones and teeth are left behind.

Drawings

Palaeontologists draw and photograph the fossils they find. Small fossils may be broken up, and the pieces can be put back together, so a drawing is made of the whole specimen, such as a skull (right).

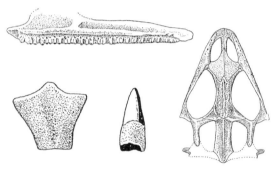

SEM scanning

The Scanning Electron Microscope (SEM) allows scientists to see great detail in tiny fossils, but also to make high-quality photographs, and even to analyse the chemical structures. It is very hard to make good photographs of tiny specimens under a normal light microscope because you can only focus on one level. In the SEM, you can see the full depth. If the preservation is unusual, some SEMs can do a chemical analysis.

Microtomograph

Palaeontologists can now 'look inside' their fossils using a microtomograph. This machine makes virtual scans through the fossil, like slicing it up, and the scans can be put together by the computer to give a 3D image of the inside. This is very useful because it avoids damaging the fossil.

SCIENTIFIC INPUT

PREPARING FOSSILS

Larger fossils are cut out of the rock in the field and wrapped in plaster and bandages to protect them. In the laboratory, the plaster parcels are cut open and the rock is carefully removed from the bones. This may require days of work with a small drill. Then each bone is coated with glues to harden it, and the whole skeleton can be assembled for display in a museum.

Dinosaur facts

Dinosaurs are well known because they broke all the records – they include the biggest land animals of all time! It can be difficult to establish accurate dinosaur measurements. Lengths are not hard, but it is very difficult to estimate weights.

LONGEST

• This is said to be *Amphicoelias*, estimated to be 40–60m long, but this dinosaur is known only from some isolated bones.

• The longest complete dinosaur that has been found is the sauropod *Supersaurus,* Late Jurassic, North America, which was 33–34m long (see pp.70–1).

• The longest predatory dinosaur was probably *Spinosaurus*, Early Cretaceous, North Africa, at some 14–18m in length, and weighing about 20 tonnes. This is much larger than *Tyrannosaurus rex*, which was 12–13m long and weighed 6–9 tonnes.

TALLEST

The tallest dinosaur was probably the sauropod *Brachiosaurus*, Late Jurassic, Tanzania (see pp.68–9), which was 25m long, but could raise its head to a height of about 13m above the ground.

HEAVIEST

• This may have been *Amphicoelias* at an estimated 120 tonnes, but this dinosaur is so incomplete that it is really impossible to be sure. More likely is the sauropod *Argentinosaurus* from the middle Cretaceous of Argentina, some 30m long, and weighing an estimated 73–88 tonnes.

SMALLEST

• This was the tiny duck-sized theropod *Mei long*, Early Cretaceous, China, measuring only 53cm in length and weighing less than 70g.

DINOSAUR EGGS

• The largest dinosaur eggs are 30cm long and 25.5cm all round, and they can hold about 3.3 litres of water. These are eggs laid by sauropod dinosaurs, and they were found in southern France and Argentina.

• The smallest dinosaur eggs were reported in 2005 from the Cretaceous of Thailand. They are 18mm long, and smaller than the eggs of a sparrow.

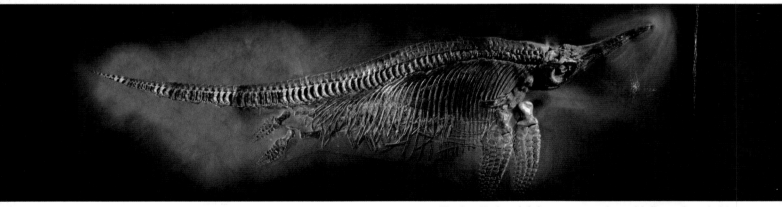

The fossil of an *Ichthyosaurus* mother with five unborn babies

WEBSITES ON RECORD-BREAKING DINOSAURS

http://en.wikipedia.org/wiki/Dinosaur_size All the records.

www.nhm.ac.uk/nature-online/life/dinosaurs-other-extinct-creatures/dino-directory/ In-depth information.

www.enchantedlearning.com/subjects/dinosaurs/questions/faq/Smallest.shtml Questions answered.

www.livescience.com/animals/060301_big_carnivores.html Dinosaurs in the news.

THE TIME OF THE GIANTS

The Late Jurassic saw the continents begin to break apart, creating smaller landmasses and the beginnings of the Atlantic Ocean. Dinosaurs continued to dominate terrestrial ecosystems, evolving into famous forms. In the sea, giant marine reptiles swam alongside ammonites, and in the air, pterosaurs began to share their habitat with a new type of dinosaur – birds.

Jurassic giants

Brachiosaurids were some of the largest Late Jurassic sauropods. Thick, spoon-shaped teeth meant this group of sauropods could break off tough plants.

Brachiosaurus was the first brachiosaur to be found and was unearthed in North America in 1903. Later expeditions to Tanzania (see pp.68–69) found additional material belonging to a similar animal.

Fossil skull

Brachiosaurs skull were full of holes, including a crest that formed two large spaces for its airways. Their big size meant these dinosaurs, like other giant sauropods, were in danger of overheating. To keep their brain cool, the skull was full of enlarged blood vessels to help shed excess heat.

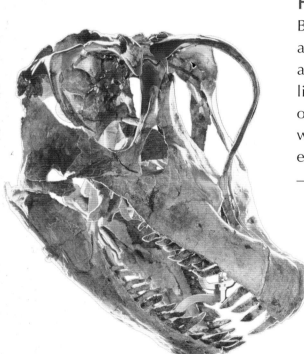

Like many of its sauropod cousins, *Brachiosaurus'* neck bones were filled with air pockets, which helped lighten the neck.

The neck and head were held out in front of the dinosaur, but could stretch up as high as 13m to reach leaves in tall trees.

Land or water?

Early palaeontologists thought *Brachiosaurus* lived in water in order to help support its bulk, using its crest as a snorkel. However, new evidence shows it lived on land – its hand bones were arranged in a semi-circle and had adapted to bear its weight.

Displaying the bones

Expeditions to Tanzania unearthed a giant sauropod that was thought to be a new species of *Brachiosaurus*. It later turned out to be a closely related but different sauropod, *Giraffatitan*. A mount of this animal can be seen in Berlin, Germany today.

Dinosaurs of Tanzania

The Tendaguru deposits in Tanzania have produced an amazing series of dinosaur skeletons. The Late Jurassic Fauna of Tanzania was similar to other locations in Europe and North America.

Geologists had reported huge bones around a hill called Tendaguru, and in 1907–13, Berlin's Natural History Museum ran expeditions.

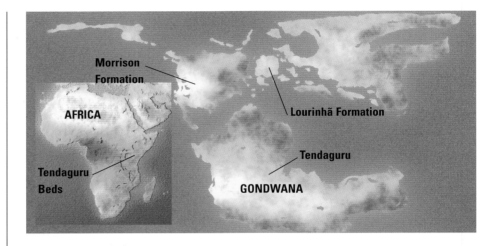

Tendaguru on the map

Today, the Tendaguru deposits lies near the East coast of Africa, however in the Late Jurassic, the continents had only just started to break away from one another. The Tendaguru contains many of the dinosaur families seen in the Morrison Formation of North America and Lourinhã Formation of Portugal. These dinosaurs may have crossed continents during periods of low sea levels.

Werner Janensch

The Tendaguru expeditions were led by Werner Janensch (1878–1969), curator at the Natural History Museum of Berlin. He spent 50 years studying the new dinosaurs that had been found.

Kentrosaurus

Kentrosaurus was a large, spiky stegosaur that was closely related to its better known North American cousin *Stegosaurus*. Its tail could swing in a wide arc and predators likely thought twice before attacking an adult.

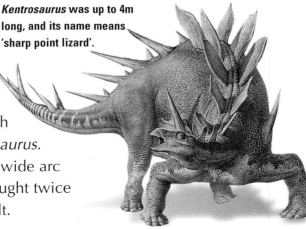

Kentrosaurus was up to 4m long, and its name means 'sharp point lizard'.

Elaphrosaurus

One of the more unusual theropods from Tendaguru is *Elaphrosaurus*, named by Janensch in 1920. This slender, 6m-long theropod may have been a fast runner and have had an omnivorous or even completely herbivorous diet.

Dicraeosaurus

Dicraeosaurus was not as big as *Giraffatitan* (p. 67), and had a relatively short neck. It likely fed on the low-lying vegetation, unlike some of its cousins that could reach higher into the trees, meaning it could avoid competition for food.

Tendaguru ecosystem

Late Jurassic Tendaguru was originally near a tidal coastline. As well as dinosaurs, pterosaurs, crocodilian relatives and ancient mammalian cousins all lived in this environment.

Dicraeosaurus could feed on short shrubs and trees measuring around 3m tall.

Dicraeosaurus reached up to 12m in height and 7 tonnes.

THE BIGGEST DINOSAURS

THE SAUROPODS WERE THE BIGGEST DINOSAURS — SOME MAY HAVE WEIGHED OVER 80 TONNES. THE BIGGEST ELEPHANT TODAY WEIGHS 6 TONNES, SO SOME WERE OVER TEN TIMES BIGGER!

EVOLUTION OF GIANTS

Sauropods became the largest land animals thanks to a range of adaptations. Moving from two legs to four early in their evolution meant their necks could get longer, which allowed them to gather more food whilst standing in the same spot; this helped to save energy for growth. They also didn't waste energy chewing food, or looking after young, and probably had efficient lungs to absorb plenty of oxygen to help power their tissues.

Growing up to 33m in length, *Diplodocus* (right) was one of the longest land animals to have lived. It ate huge amounts of food, using its long neck to reach high vegetation.

- **Amphicoelias**
- **Diplodocus**
- **Supersaurus**
- **Bruhathkayosaurus**
- **Argentinosaurus**
- **Sauroposeidon**

PARADE OF THE GIANTS

Ranging from 6m to around 60m, the debate over which sauropod was the longest and largest continues today. Many skeletons are incomplete, making direct comparisons difficult. The titanosaurs like *Argentinosaurus* and *Patagotitan* are generally thought to be the biggest, however there are remains of giants that may have dwarfed them. More research is required before we can crown the biggest animal to ever walk Earth.

Bone wars

For over 20 years, two 19th Century palaeontologists, rushing to be the first to name new animal, scrapped over all the new dinosaur fossils found in the western USA.

Cope and Marsh began as friends, working together until 1870. Then they squabbled over the rights to a particular dig site, and their teams came to blows.

Othniel Charles Marsh

Marsh (right, on the left) was a professor at Yale University. He named 80 new species of dinosaurs, including *Allosaurus* and *Diplodocus*, as well as the Cretaceous bird *Ichthyornis*.

Edward Drinker Cope

Cope published over 1,300 scientific papers, discovering and describing thousands of new species of modern and extinct animals. He named several dinosaurs, including *Camarasaurus* and *Coelophysis*.

Early field teams

Marsh and Cope paid railroad men, and others, to dig up bones. These men put them in wooden crates and sent them back east by railroad. There was no time to map the site or protect the bones.

Apatosaurus

Marsh named *Apatosaurus* in 1877, based on some isolated bones of a huge animal from the Morrison Formation (see pp.74–5). It had a thick neck, which some scientists argue may have been used during tussles between pairs of angry *Apatosaurus*.

Brontosaurus

Marsh found another large sauropod in 1879, which he named *Brontosaurus*, or 'thunder lizard'. A few years later, other researchers argued it was no different to *Apatosaurus*. It wasn't until 2015 that scientist revisited the bones and agreed *Brontosaurus* was a genuine type of dinosaur!

Damaged legacy

The intense rivalry between the two fossil hunters affected their research. Bones were incorrectly assembled or described, whilst the use of dynamite destroyed fossil sites.

HISTORICAL DATA

ARMED TO THE TEETH

The 1870s and 1880s were still the days of the 'Wild West', and the fossil diggers had to go armed with rifles. This picture shows Marsh – he is the bearded man in the centre of the back row – with his team. These hardy men slept in tents, even in the freezing winters. Marsh paid them by results, and they had to fight off bad weather, grizzly bears and rival bone-diggers.

THE MORRISON FORMATION

The Morrison Formation of the Midwestern USA has been one of the richest sources of dinosaur fossils since the 'bone wars' began in the 1870s (see pp.72–3).

MORRISON MAMMALS

The Morrison Formation has not only yielded specimens of dinosaurs, but also plants, fishes and other land animals. The Morrison mammals and their close cousins include several small, shrew-like animals with sharp, needle-like teeth. They probably hunted insects such as beetles.

MORRISON ROCKS

The rocks of the Morrison Formation are sandstones and mudstones, mainly deposited by ancient rivers. Dinosaur skeletons are mostly found in ancient sand bars, deposits of sand in the middle of rivers. When heavy rains fell, the rivers became raging torrents, and dead animals and plants were swept away. As the flow slowed, the remains were dumped on sand banks at the edges and in the middle of the rivers.

MORRISON LANDSCAPE

Allosaurus, *Diplodocus*, *Stegosaurus* and *Ornitholestes* (below) fossils have all been found among the Morrison Formation. They would have moved and hunted about on the river plain surrounded by a lush vegetation of horsetails and ferns in the marshy areas, and ginkgo and conifer trees on more stable ground.

Stegosaurus

Stegosaurus is one of the best-known dinosaurs found in the Morrison Formation. It was one of the first armoured, plant-eating dinosaurs to be studied in detail.

The plates down its back have caused endless debate. They did not protect its sides, but they made it look bigger. They were probably covered in skin.

Reconstruction

At one time, palaeontologists wondered whether there was a single row of plates, or whether they stood out sideways, forming a kind of bony sunshade. New specimens show their upright pattern, and the short arms show that the head was carried close to the ground, while the tail was raised quite high.

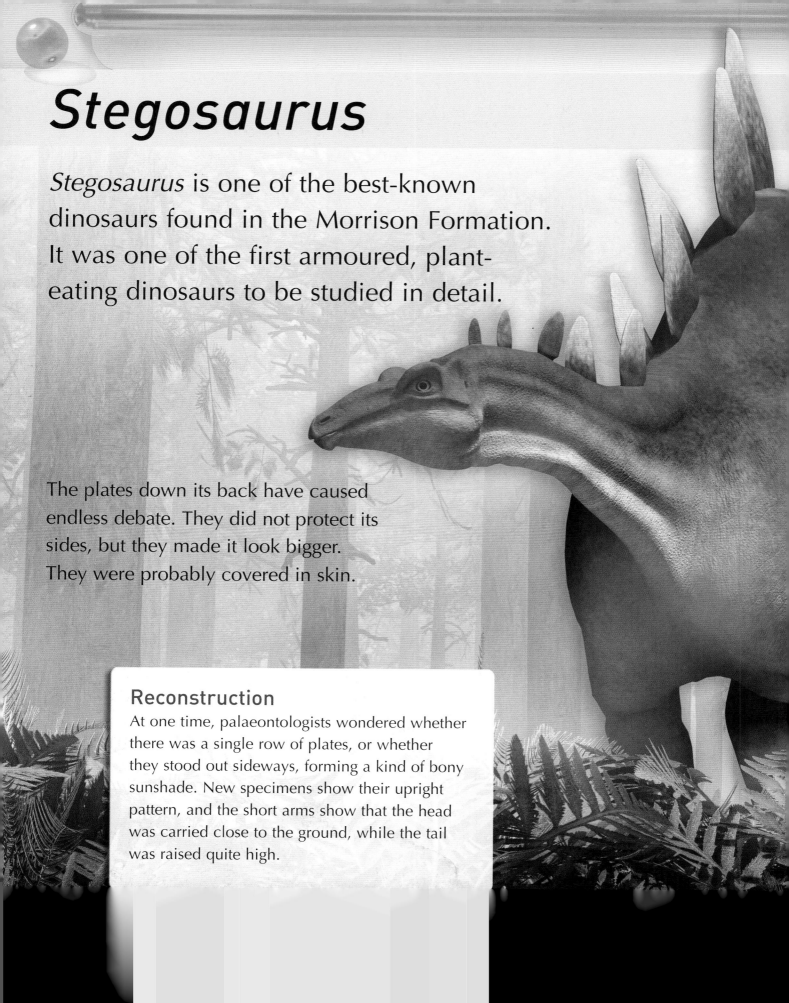

Stegosaurus' plates were covered in a keratin sheath (the same substance in claws and beaks). Pipe-like canals inside the plates were full of blood vessels.

Armoured plates

The bony plates began behind the head, and ran down the back to spikes at the end of the tail. Each plate stood in the skin and muscle of the back – not connected to the backbone. They were probably upright, and could not be moved about.

Stegosaurus had a tiny, tubular skull and jaws lined with small, leaf-shaped teeth for snipping plants.

Different dinosaurs had different weapons on their tails. Ankylosaurs sometimes had great bony clubs for hitting their enemies. *Stegosaurus* had sharp spikes on its tail, probably also for defence.

Stegosaurus and its cousins show adaptations to weight bearing similar to sauropod dinosaurs. Their hand bones were arranged in a semi-circle, like a pillar, to help support the weight of their bodies.

Allosaurus

One of the most common and famous Late Jurassic carnivores, *Allosaurus* stalked the floodplains of North America and Europe.

Well-preserved fossils show that theropods such as *Allosaurus* ate meat and allowed researchers to study this theropod in detail.

Fossil tooth
Allosaurus had curved teeth with a pointed tip and a serrated edge front and back, like the edge of a steak knife.

MEASURING FORCES
Finite element analysis is a technique used by engineers to test the strength of bridges and buildings, but it can be used on animals, too.

The skull is scanned into a computer using a laser scanner.

The skull scan is converted into a 3D mesh of imaginary cells.

Forces are applied to the mesh's cells to test how the skull behaves.

Stresses and strains
Finite element analysis (left) allows palaeontologists to model the forces on dinosaur skulls. This computer model shows the effects of biting on *Allosaurus'* skull. The 'colder colours' (blues and greens) show the areas of high compression during biting.

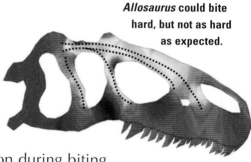

Allosaurus could bite hard, but not as hard as expected.

Allosaurus attack
Although *Allosaurus* had a weaker bite than expected, its skull was adapted to withstand large forces. It may have used its neck muscles and impressive jaws to drive its skull into prey rather than bite hard.

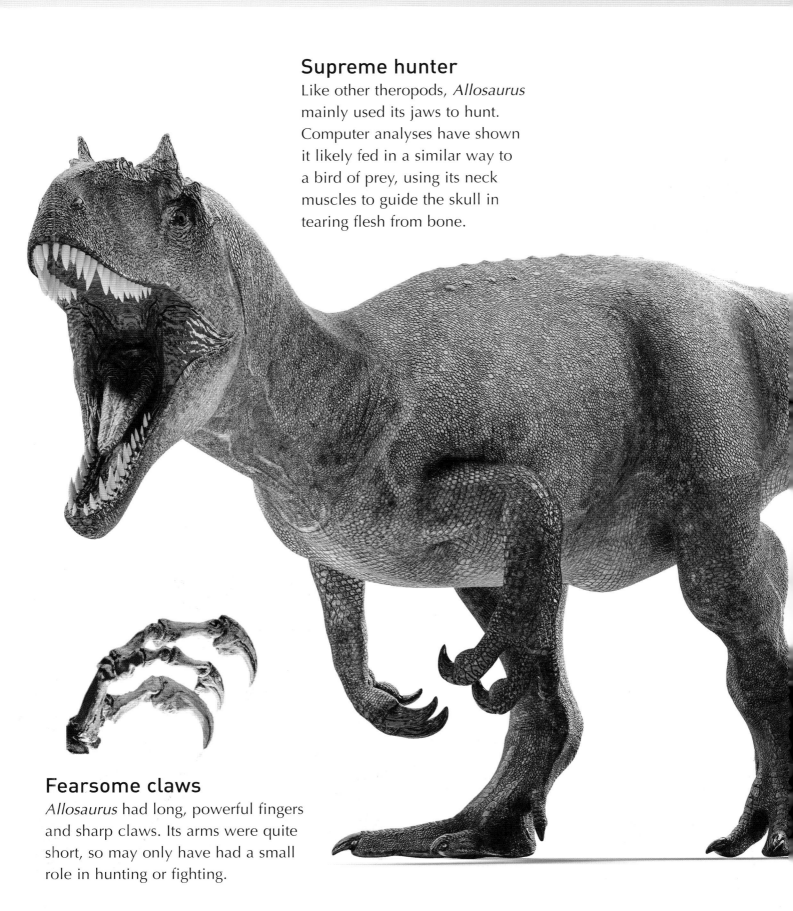

Supreme hunter

Like other theropods, *Allosaurus* mainly used its jaws to hunt. Computer analyses have shown it likely fed in a similar way to a bird of prey, using its neck muscles to guide the skull in tearing flesh from bone.

Fearsome claws

Allosaurus had long, powerful fingers and sharp claws. Its arms were quite short, so may only have had a small role in hunting or fighting.

DINOSAURS AND DRIFT

DINOSAURS ORIGINATED ON A SINGLE SUPERCONTINENT CALLED PANGAEA. THE ATLANTIC OCEAN BEGAN TO OPEN UP DURING THE JURASSIC AND CRETACEOUS. THE SCIENTIFIC EVIDENCE FOR CONTINENTAL DRIFT IS OVERWHELMING.

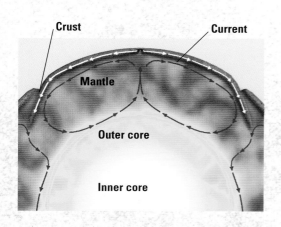

Crust
Current
Mantle
Outer core
Inner core

WHY PLATES PART

Earth has a rocky outer crust divided into various plates. Inside the planet, hot molten core and mantle create great currents, which moves the plates above. Sometimes they spread apart, sometimes they collide, helping shape the land and seas over thousands of years.

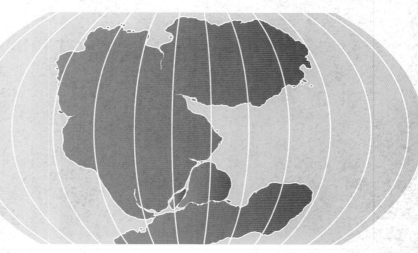

TRIASSIC
All of Earth's land was joined up in one supercontinent called Pangea.

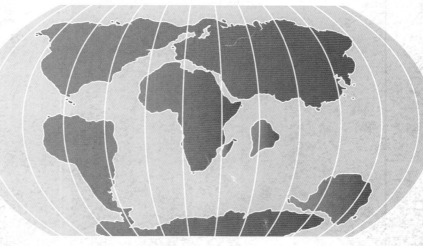

CRETACEOUS
The continents drifted further apart. The sea level was higher and North America and Africa were both split by sea. Europe and Asia were broken up into islands.

SHARED FAUNA

One of the key pieces of evidence for continental drift is the distribution of fossils. *Lystrosaurus*, a primitive mammalian relative from the Triassic, and *Mesosaurus*, a semi aquatic reptile from the Early Permian, have been found on multiple continents.

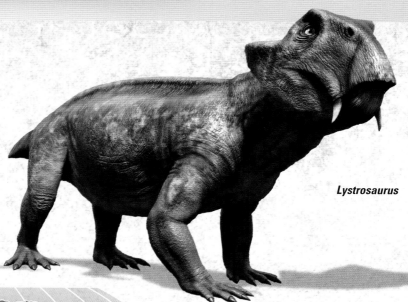

Lystrosaurus

JURASSIC

During the Jurassic, there were two main continents – Laurasia in the north and Gondwana in the south.

THEN AND NOW

These maps show the world in the Triassic, Jurassic, Cretaceous and the present day. In the Jurassic, the southern supercontinent Gondwana is still present, but the South Atlantic opened up in the Cretaceous, separating South America and Africa. India also began to drift off towards the rest of Asia, and Australia and Antarctica broke away.

Mesosaurus

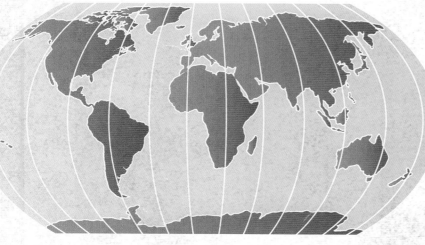

TODAY

The Solnhofen lagoon

The details of ancient life often come from unique sites where delicate fossils have been preserved. The Solnhofen lagoon of southern Germany opens a window in time to Jurassic life.

MAKING A PRINT

About 200 years ago, printers invented the process of lithography, which means 'printing from stone'.

A drawing is made on the smooth limestone surface using oily ink or paint.

Ink is spread over the stone, but it sticks only to the oily drawing.

Paper is laid over the stone in a press, and picks up the image.

Each lithographic stone can make thousands of copies of a drawing.

Stonemasons found the first fossils in Solnhofen hundreds of years ago. The site was made famous by the discovery of the early bird *Archaeopteryx*.

The lagoon

The rocks at Solnhofen are limestones. There are fossils of animals that lived in the surrounding, warm seas, as well as some land plants, rare dinosaurs, insects, birds and pterosaurs.

The Solnhofen quarries

German stonemasons have been extracting thin limestone slabs from the Solnhofen quarries for centuries. The slabs are so fine-grained that, in the past, they have been used for printing (see left). Today, they are used for building.

Fossil finds

The limestone rocks were initially deposited as mud silts. This type of sediment means that fossils can be preserved in exquisite conditions. When split, some slabs have a beautiful impression of the fossil on both halves, like this fish (above).

Salty waters

The lagoon waters were extremely salty and inhospitable to life. Animals would have washed or fallen into the lagoon and sank to the bottom. The lack of scavengers and decomposers prevented the bodies from getting broken up or destroyed.

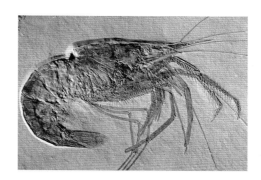

Compsognathus

A rare dinosaur from Solnhofen is *Compsognathus*, a small flesh-eater, known from a few specimens that was found in 1859. This delicate, 1m-long animal fed on small prey, such as lizards or mammals on land.

This original specimen of *Compsognathus* is complete, and shows the head bending back over the body.

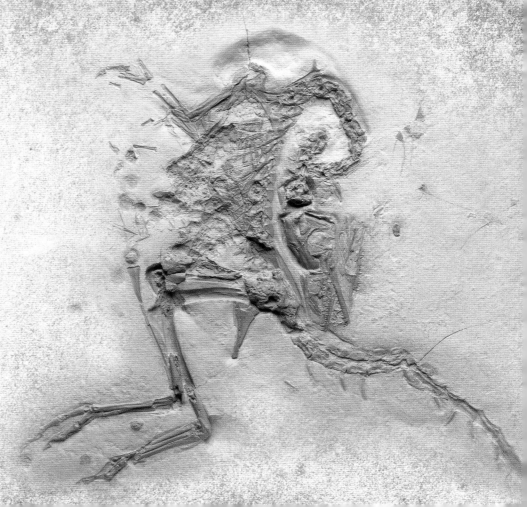

Archaeopteryx

The most famous fossil in the world is probably that of *Archaeopteryx*, considered by many to be the first bird.

The first fossils of this 'early bird' were found in 1860 in Solnhofen, Germany. Since then, twelve fossil skeletons from the Late Jurassic have been discovered, also in Germany.

The first bird

Palaeontologists have debated for years how well *Archaeopteryx* could fly. Analyses of the arm bones revealed that *Archaeopteryx* was likely capable of flight, but in a way unseen in modern birds.

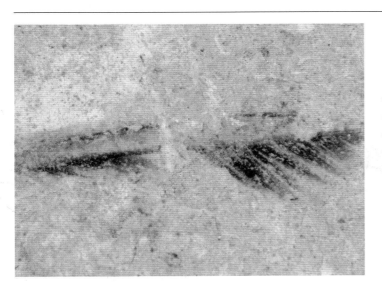

This 150-million-year-old feather was discovered in Germany.

Feather colours

Fossilized pigments were detected in a feather found at Solnhofen, suggesting that *Archaeopteryx* once had black in its feathers. However, this suggestion has been countered by other scientists.

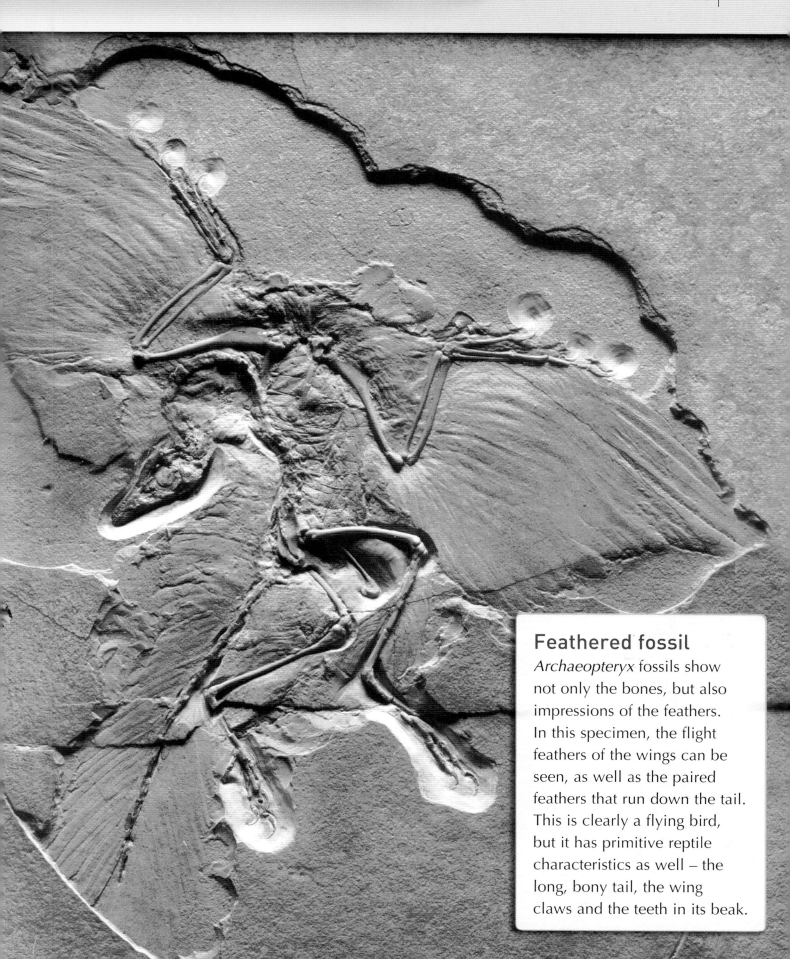

Feathered fossil

Archaeopteryx fossils show not only the bones, but also impressions of the feathers. In this specimen, the flight feathers of the wings can be seen, as well as the paired feathers that run down the tail. This is clearly a flying bird, but it has primitive reptile characteristics as well – the long, bony tail, the wing claws and the teeth in its beak.

FLYING REPTILES

PTEROSAURS WERE EXTRAORDINARY REPTILES, CLOSE RELATIVES OF THE DINOSAURS. THEY ALSO EVOLVED DURING THE TRIASSIC AND WERE THE DOMINANT FLYING VERTEBRATE DURING THE MESOZOIC. PTEROSAURS HAD LONG WINGS FORMED BY AN EXTENDED FOURTH FINGER ON THE HAND, WHICH SUPPORTED A THIN, FLEXIBLE WING MADE FROM SKIN.

FOSSIL FINDS

Some of the best specimens of pterosaurs are known from the Solnhofen lagoon of the Late Jurassic. They were found in the same rocks as *Archaeopteryx* (see pp.84–5). Some specimens, such as *Rhamphorhynchus* (above), shows the delicate skeleton, as well as clear impressions of the wing membranes. The wings were made from several layers of skin, with muscle and blood vessels, and the body was covered with hair-like fibres.

PTEROSAURS OF THE LAGOON

The first Solnhofen pterosaur specimen was reported in 1784. Since then, hundreds of specimens have been found, and many named. Several types of pterosaur soared over the lagoons and warm seas near modern day Solnhofen, ranging in size from a blackbird to a large seagull. Most fed on small prey, such as fish and invertebrates. Fossil footprints show that they walked on all fours, their wings folded against their body.

Dinosaurs of Portugal

The Lourinhã Formation of Portugal is rich in dinosaur fossils. They show that the country shared dinosaurs not only with the rest of Europe, but also with North America.

The dinosaur fauna found in these Late Jurassic rocks were similar to those of the Morrison formation, suggesting a land bridge once connected Europe and North America.

Lourinhanosaurus

A partial skeleton of this flesh-eater was found in 1998. It could be related to *Allosaurus* from North America, or to *Megalosaurus* from England – no one is sure. It is important not to confuse *Lourinhanosaurus* with *Lourinhasaurus*, a sauropod that is also from Portugal.

Dinheirosaurus

Many sauropods have been found in Portugal, but most of the finds are only of parts of the skeleton. *Dinheirosaurus* was named in 1999, based on a series of vertebrae from its spine (below). The vertebrae are like those from the backbone of *Diplodocus*.

The spikes along the tail were fixed deep into the skin and muscle, and would have deterred predators.

Dacentrurus

By the Late Jurassic, stegosaurs were known worldwide (see pp.76–7). *Dacentrurus* is a stegosaur that has been unearthed in several parts of Europe, and it was found in Portugal in the 1990s. The armour consists of small plates at the front, and long spikes further back.

Torvosaurus probably held its prey down with its massive, three-toed feet as it tore at the flesh with its jaws.

Octavio Mateus

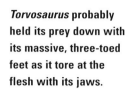

Mateus has run dinosaur excavations in Portugal since 1991, mainly near the town of Lourinha. His work has revealed a whole new dinosaur fauna that was barely known before, and he has named seven new dinosaurs.

Footprints by the shore

There are many long dinosaur trackways in late Jurassic rocks along Portugal's Atlantic coastline. Here, Octavio Mateus is pointing to a series of footprints, one of the 17 trackways found at this site.

Torvosaurus

When *Torvosaurus* was found in Portugal, it was already known from the Morrison Formation. A temporary land bridge across the proto-Atlantic Ocean helped dinosaurs migrate across both continents. This giant predator weighed at least 4 tonnes and is the largest theropod found in Europe.

EARTH EVIDENCE

A YOUNG PALAEONTOLOGIST

Palaeontologists of all ages can make great discoveries. Eleven-year-old Jacob Walen of the Netherlands is holding a piece of a dinosaur's jaw bone next to a reconstructed skull of *Torvosaurus* at the Lourinha Museum. He found the jawbone in 2003, when he was only six, while on holiday in Portugal with his family, and gave the fossil to the museum in 2008. His discovery is now famous – it was reported all around the world.

Marine life

The Late Jurassic was teeming with marine creatures. Ichthyosaurs and crocodile cousins hunted fishes and squid, and in turn were eaten by large pliosaurs.

Fossils of these remarkable animals have been found in many parts of the world. Some have the remains of their last meal in their stomachs.

Liopleurodon

Estimates of *Liopleurdon's* size have been grossly exaggerated and many modern estimates now place this powerful predator at around 5–7m on average. Huge jaws meant it could tackle big prey.

Metriorhynchus

A group of reptiles called the Thalattosuchians evolved to live life at sea. Related to modern crocodilians some, such as the 3m-long *Metriorhynchus*, modified their limbs into paddles and had a tail fin.

Fossil fish

Fish were plentiful in the Jurassic seas, ranging in shape and size. Some such as *Leedsichthys* (above), were filter-feeding giants, measuring up to 16m long. They fed on small invertebrates and plankton at the water's surface.

Pliosaurus

One of the largest predators in the Jurassic seas, *Pliosaurus* is known from several species, some of which had a devastating bite force. Some skulls measured around 3m in length and this giant could tackle prey weighing up to 2 tonnes.

Belemnites had fins at the side to keep their balance in the water as they swam.

Belemnites

These creatures are related to modern cuttlefish and squid, as well as to the fossil ammonites (see p.47). Belemnites had a shell, but it was internal and shaped like a bullet. The fleshy body had tentacles for catching food.

AMAZING FACTS

FOSSIL VOMIT

A discovery in England may be the best example of fossil vomit. Belemnite shells found in tight bunches in the rock may have been eaten by ichthyosaurs. The belemnite shells, called rostra, show signs of acid etching on their surface, indicating they had been in a predator's stomach. The rostra were indigestible, and may have damaged the hunter internally, so vomiting was an easy way to expel them.

Shaximiao Formation

The dinosaurs of the Shaximiao Formation are significant, as Middle Jurassic rocks a globally rare.

This Formation crops out in Sichuan, China, and preserves the inhabitants of an ancient forest ecosystem.

Dong Zhiming

A prolific dinosaur specialist, Dong Zhiming has named many famous Chinese dinosaurs, including most of the Jurassic dinosaurs on these pages, and was one of the first to work on the Dashanpu dig site.

Huayangosaurus was 4.5m long.

Huayangosaurus

One of Dong Zhiming's Dashanpu discoveries is the remarkable stegosaur *Huayangosaurus*. Unlike its relative *Stegosaurus* (see pp.76–7), *Huayangosaurus'* back plates were narrower and it had a broader head.

Shunosaurus

Almost every bone is known for this 10m-long sauropod, with the remains of several individuals discovered in China. Unlike *Diplodocus* and most of its cousins, it had a small club at the end of its tail, perhaps to ward off predators.

Xiaosaurus

This small, plant-eating dinosaur may be related to *Lesothosaurus* from South Africa (see p.34). It is known only from teeth and a few isolated bones, so reconstructions can't be authenticated.

Xuanhanosaurus

This theropod was 4.5m long, and likely preyed on *Xiaosaurus* and other smaller dinosaurs. *Xuanhanosaurus* had powerful arms, probably for grabbing and grappling with prey. The incomplete fossils suggest that it may be a relative of *Megalosaurus* (see pp.56–7) or *Allosaurus* (see pp.78–9).

Yangchuanosaurus's skull measure 82cm long.

Yangchuanosaurus

A large predator, *Yangchuanosaurus* is known from the Late Jurassic part of the Shaximiao Formation. This dinosaur was 8–10m long, and had short arms, with three fingers on each hand. It had a large skull, deep, powerful jaws and a low, bony crest along its snout – possibly for display.

The Zigong dinosaurs

Some of the best Chinese fossils are from the Middle Jurassic Shaximiao Formation in Zigong Province.

The first fossils were found in 1972 when a Chinese gas company found the bones of a theropod, later called *Gasosaurus.*

Gasosaurus
This theropod was up to 4m long and is a little like *Megalosaurus* (see pp.56–7). Its skull has not been found, so a reconstruction was made for display in the Zigong Museum.

Omeisaurus
There were several sauropods in the Shaximiao Formation, including *Omeisaurus*, which was up to 15m long and weighed 10 tonnes. This dinosaur was first reported in 1939, and since then many species from the Middle Jurassic have been found in different locations in China.

A gap in the record
For a long time, the Middle Jurassic was a mystery because its dinosaurs were not well known. The only finds were in Europe, and there were no discoveries in North America. The findings in Zigong Province in the 1970s filled the gap, and showed that China had similar dinosaurs to those found in England.

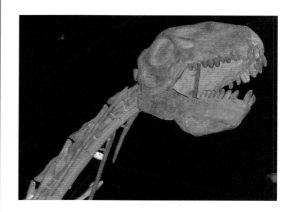

Datousaurus
This sauropod was also 15m long. It had a relatively large skull, with spoon-shaped teeth in the jaws. Its name means 'big head reptile'. *Datousaurus* and *Omeisaurus* may have fed on different plants, so they would not have been in competition.

The Zigong Dinosaur Museum

One of the most amazing dinosaur displays is in Zigong, where the palaeontologists decided to preserve part of the original bone bed as a permanent exhibit. They found so many bones in one place that a roof could be built over the dinosaur graveyard. Visitors can see the technicians cleaning up the bones where they lie.

Dinosaur facts

About 1,500 species of dinosaurs have been named since 1824, and a new dinosaur is named every two or three weeks. Many of the older identifications turn out to be incorrect, or are based on remains that cannot be identified.

THE FIRST DINOSAUR
• The oldest confirmed fossils *Saturnalia, Staurikosaurus, Pampadromaeus, Buriolestes* (233 MYA), from the Santa Maria formation.

THE LAST DINOSAURS
• Fossils of *Tyrannosaurus rex* and *Triceratops* are found in the last few metres of the Hell Creek Formation, Montana, USA, in the Cretaceous, just below the great mass extinction level (see p.149).

SHORTEST DINOSAUR NAME
• *Yi qi*, which means 'strange wing'. This was a small type of theropod with an elongated third finger and special wrist that may have supported a bat-like wing membrane.

LONGEST DINOSAUR NAME
• *Micropachycephalosaurus hongtuyanensis*, which means 'tiny thick-headed reptile from Hongtuyan'. Possibly a ceratopsian dinosaur from the Late Cretaceous of China, it was named by the Chinese palaeontologist Dong Zhiming in 1978.

FIRST DINOSAUR TO BE NAMED
• *Megalosaurus*, which was named by William Buckland in 1824. This was a large theropod from the Middle Jurassic of England.

LAST DINOSAUR TO BE NAMED
It is impossible to say because a new dinosaur species is named about every two weeks somewhere in the world. Type in 'new dinosaur, this month', in any search engine and see what comes up!

A *Diplodocus* from Wyoming, USA, originally described by palaeontologist OC Marsh

WEBSITES ON THE HISTORY OF PALAEONTOLOGISTS AND DINOSAUR NAMING

http://palaeo.gly.bris.ac.uk/Palaeofiles/History/index.html   All the historical dinosaur hunters.

http://academic.brooklyn.cuny.edu/geology/chamber/dinohist1.html   More on dinosaur hunters.

http://en.wikipedia.org/wiki/Portal:Dinosaurs   Access to information on many dinosaurs.

http://en.wikipedia.org/wiki/List_of_dinosaurs   Check this list for the latest dinosaurs.

A MODERNIZING WORLD

The early Cretaceous saw the continents begin to fragment substantially. On land, relatives of bees hovered around the dinosaurs, pollinating an increasingly flowering world. In the sea, marine reptiles still dominated, whilst birds enjoyed life in the air.

The Wealden scene

Early examples of the new ecosystems may be seen in the Early Cretaceous of southeast England, in rocks called the Wealden Group.

The Cretaceous was warmer than today, with high levels of CO_2 and other gases in the atmosphere keeping conditions balmy. The poles lacked ice caps, but may have been frosty during the winter.

The Wealden scene

There were still sauropods, but the landscape was dominated by ornithopod dinosaurs, such as *Iguanodon* and *Mantellisaurus*, that browsed on low plants. There was also a new predator – *Baryonyx*, a long-snouted spinosaurid (above).

The Wealden in the UK

The Wealden rocks are to be seen south of London (right). Geologists have studied them for hundreds of years, and the first dinosaur bones were found in the 1820s. Since then, palaeontologists have found thousands of fossil plants, mammals, fishes, lizards, shellfish and dinosaurs.

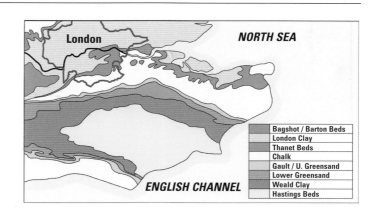

London

NORTH SEA

ENGLISH CHANNEL

| Bagshot / Barton Beds |
| London Clay |
| Thanet Beds |
| Chalk |
| Gault / U. Greensand |
| Lower Greensand |
| Weald Clay |
| Hastings Beds |

Wealden plants

Dozens of different plant fossils have been found in the Wealden rocks. Low-growing ferns and horsetails grew in damp areas beside rivers and ponds, together with bushy and tree-like plants such as cycads, ginkgos and conifers. This fossil frond (left) is named *Zamites*. It was a cycad that looked like a giant pineapple, and it had dozens of fronds sprouting from the top.

Wealden prints

Wealden fossils include footprints, as well as burrows made by shrimps and shellfish. This three-toed dinosaur footprint was probably made by *Iguanodon*, when the dinosaur stepped in some soft sand.

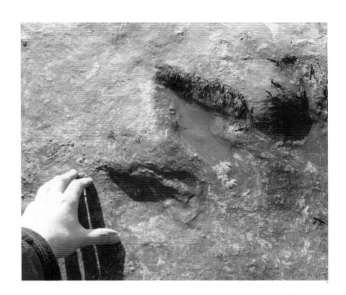

Fossil finds

The Wealden rocks were mainly laid down in rivers and lakes. Some of the fish, such as *Scheenstia* (left), were quite large. This fish was up to 50cm long and had regular rows of thick, squarish, bony scales. Even with such an armour, there is evidence the dinosaur *Baryonyx* ate it.

Iguanodon

Iguanodon was the first plant-eating dinosaur ever named. Its teeth showed it was a plant-eater.

Unlike flesh-eating dinosaurs – which have sharp, pointed, curved teeth – *Iguanodon* has rather blunt and broad teeth. But did it walk on all fours or on its hind legs?

Thumb spike

With so few bones to work from, Mantell had no idea what *Iguanodon* looked like. He thought it was a giant lizard that had a horn on its snout. Further studies from the 1870s discoveries revealed that Mantell's 'nose horn' was actually a thumb spike.

Gideon Mantell

Iguanodon was named by Sussex doctor Gideon Mantell (1790–1852), after his wife Mary purchased some of its teeth for him. It was only the second dinosaur ever named, after *Megalosaurus* (see pp.56–7).

A social animal

The study of over thirty *Iguanodon* specimens found in a Belgian coal mine during the 1870s, suggested this herbivore lived in herds and walked on all fours.

Reconstructing *Iguanodon*
After the discoveries in Belgium, the new skeletons were set up for a great display at the Natural History Museum in the capital, Brussels. Each skeleton was carefully wired together, and held up on great metal frameworks. However, the two-legged pose is incorrect, and scientists think the fused wrists and bulky arm bones meant *Iguanodon* mainly walked on all fours.

HYPSILOPHODON

One of the Wealden dinosaurs (see p.99) was a small ornithischian called *Hypsilophodon*. It was named in 1869, and several skeletons of this 2.3m-long plant-eater have been found.

ANATOMY OF THE JAWS

Hypsilophodon had a short snout and rows of peg-like teeth in its jaws. There was a set of teeth near the front of the mouth that was used for snipping leaves and fronds, and a row further back that was used for chewing. A beak covered the front of the jaw. The toothy tip of the upper jaw is unusual for a Cretaceous ornithischian, as this trait had generally been lost by then in favour of the beak.

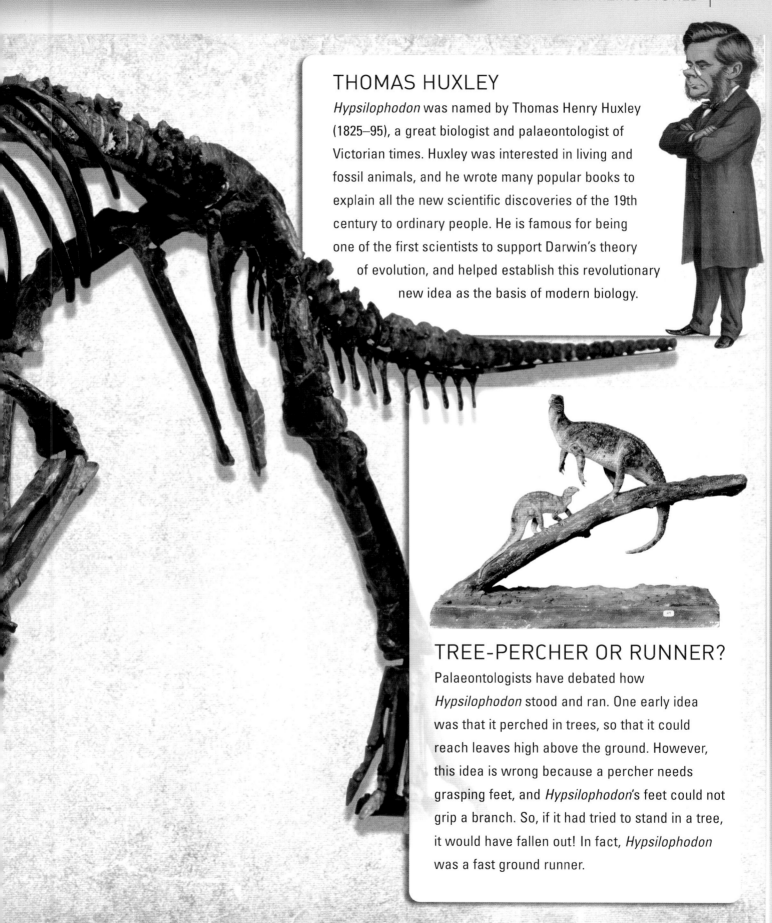

THOMAS HUXLEY

Hypsilophodon was named by Thomas Henry Huxley (1825–95), a great biologist and palaeontologist of Victorian times. Huxley was interested in living and fossil animals, and he wrote many popular books to explain all the new scientific discoveries of the 19th century to ordinary people. He is famous for being one of the first scientists to support Darwin's theory of evolution, and helped establish this revolutionary new idea as the basis of modern biology.

TREE-PERCHER OR RUNNER?

Palaeontologists have debated how *Hypsilophodon* stood and ran. One early idea was that it perched in trees, so that it could reach leaves high above the ground. However, this idea is wrong because a percher needs grasping feet, and *Hypsilophodon*'s feet could not grip a branch. So, if it had tried to stand in a tree, it would have fallen out! In fact, *Hypsilophodon* was a fast ground runner.

Ornithopods

Ornithopods like *Iguanodon* were a hugely successful group of herbivores during the Cretaceous.

They first appeared in the Jurassic and they went on to evolve extremely complex teeth that helped them tackle all kinds of plant matter.

Evolution and adaptation

Ornithopods were uncommon during the Jurassic, even in fossil rich rocks such as those of the Morrison Formation (pp.74–5). Several Cretaceous groups became large and mainly quadrupedal, their wrist bones fusing to support their weight on their hands. One group of Cretaceous ornithopods, the hadrosaurs, grew showy crests for display.

Body size

Most of the known early ornithopods were small to mid-sized – *Gideonmantellia*, for example was around 1 metre long. However, some of the Cretaceous ornithopods were huge. *Shantungosaurus* (left) measured over 15m in length, with a thigh bone that was as tall as a man.

Shantungosaurus could weigh up to 16 tonnes.

Tenontosaurus

Tenontosaurus was a North American relative of *Iguanodon* and lived during the Early Cretaceous. It had a very long tail for its size, giving it an overall length of around 7m.

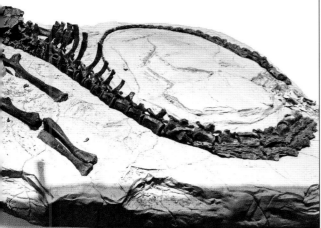

Early reconstruction of *Iguanodon* in the squatting or 'kangaroo' posture.

Posture

Some early reconstructions showed ornithopods with the body upright and the hind legs tucked back. Whilst early forms were likely bipedal, later ornithopods transitioned to a mainly four-legged way of moving around, although they may have reared up onto their hind legs from time to time.

Ouranosaurus

Ouranosaurus was a very peculiar ornithopod. Closely related to *Iguanodon*, this 8m-long herbivore also sported an immense sail down its back and tail. Found in the deserts of Niger, in Africa, the sail may have been used for display.

Iguanodon's hand and thumb

Iguanodon's hand was modified for walking. The middle three toes sported small, hood-like claws, and the fused wrist helped support its weight. The outer finger was relatively mobile, unlike the conical thumb spike. Scientists still don't know what it's purpose.

It has been suggested the thumb spike was a weapon, but this idea is difficult to prove.

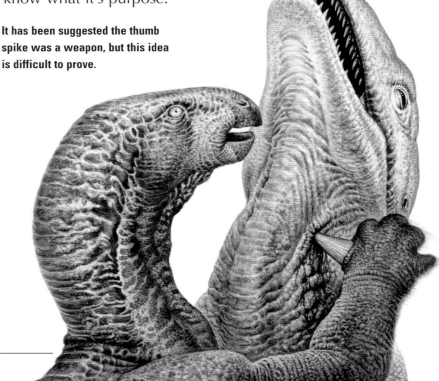

Liaoning Province

In the last thirty years, one area in northeast China has become famous for Early Cretaceous fossil finds.

The Jehol Group of Liaoning Province, and surrounding areas, has produced some of the most amazing fossils ever unearthed. They include dinosaurs with feathers!

Amadeus Grabau

Grabau (1870–1946), a German-American palaeontologist, was one of the first westerners to be allowed to work in China. He was appointed professor at Peking National University and was chief palaeontologist for the Chinese Geological Survey.

Fossil rocks

The Jehol Biota represents life from several fossil-rich rock formations, which date back to the Early Cretaceous. Many of the fossils were quickly buried in soft sediments, allowing exquisite preservation.

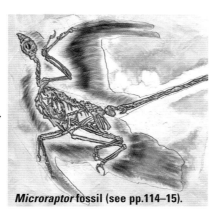

Microraptor fossil (see pp.114–15).

Large eye socket shows dinosaur had excellent vision

Fossil find

This skull is 11cm long and belonged to a theropod dinosaur that had distinctive front teeth like those of a rodent. Named *Incisivosaurus* (see p.111), which means 'incisor lizard', it was collected from the lowermost (earliest) levels of the Yixian Formation in western Liaoning.

Excavating fossils

Thousands of fossils have been excavated from the Jehol Group by Chinese palaeontologists. Some of the fossils come out of deep mines, dug out by workers as they follow a particularly fossil-rich rock layer. In other cases, the palaeontologists open a quarry like this one, and work down layer by layer.

Land rich in fossils

The Liaoning landscape's gentle, rolling hills are covered with fields. When the farmers dig for road stone, they find fossils everywhere.

FLOWERS FLOURISH

ONE OF THE MOST REMARKABLE EVENTS WAS THE EVOLUTION OF FLOWERING PLANTS. IN THE EARLY CRETACEOUS, THEY BEGAN TO BECOME ESTABLISHED AROUND THE WORLD. BY THE END OF THE CRETACEOUS, THEY HAD TAKEN OVER.

FOSSIL FINDS

One of the oldest fossil flowers, this specimen of *Archaefructus* comes from the Early Cretaceous of Liaoning Province in China. This flower was found in the same rocks as the remarkable specimens of birds and dinosaurs with feathers (see pp.116–17), but it is not clear whether those dinosaurs ate such plants.

ANATOMY OF A FLOWER

The new plant groups of the Cretaceous had flowers, unlike more ancient groups such as ferns, cycads and conifers. The flower evolved as a device to spread pollen, either by wind or on the bodies of pollinating animals. The pollen is produced by stamens and is deposited on the pistil in the middle of the flower, where sperm passes down to fertilize the developing seeds. The seeds ripen, the flower withers, and the seeds are then scattered on the ground where many new plants may grow.

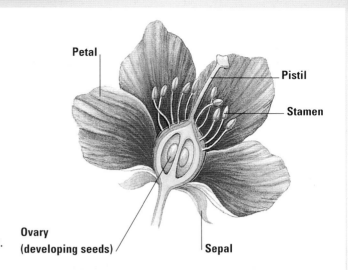

Petal
Pistil
Stamen
Ovary
(developing seeds)
Sepal

TERRESTRIAL REVOLUTION

The flowering plants scientists know of were small and rare when they first appeared some 125 million years ago. But their new way of breeding, involving flowers and pollination, gave them great advantages as they could photosynthesize more efficiently. Slowly, through the rest of the Cretaceous, flowering plants began to dominate. Their pollinators were insect groups such as bees, beetles and ants. This remarkable revolution marked the beginning of modern terrestrial ecosystems.

Feathered dinosaurs

The Jehol fossil beds of China give us a remarkable insight into life in the Early Cretaceous. Dinosaurs, birds and mammals can all be found.

The Jehol rocks were deposited mainly in lakes (see pp.106–7), and preserve beautifully delicate tissues, such as feathers.

Sinosauropteryx

This little theropod was the first non-bird dinosaur to be found with evidence of feathers. Preserved pigments in the feathers suggest it may have been reddish brown on top with a pale underbelly, as well as having a banded tail.

Beipiaosaurus

Beipiaosaurus is a therizinosaur, one of a group of plant-eating theropods (see pp.136–7). This medium-sized dinosaur, 2.2m long, had two main types of feathers – short down feathers and long, filament-like feathers, up to 15cm in length, which covered the head, neck and chest, and also behind its arms.

Dilong

When *Dilong* was named in 2004, it was identified as an early tyrannosauroid, an ancient cousin of the more famous *Tyrannosaurus*. It sported short, simple feathers that were likely an adaptation to keep warm. Brain scans suggest it was good at tracking moving objects.

The name *Dilong* means 'emperor dragon', and only one species has been found.

Chinese palaeontologist Xu Xing found and named *Sinornithosaurus*.

Sinornithosaurus

This was a dromaeosaurid – a group of theropods that includes *Deinonychus* (see pp.120–1). Long arm feathers likely stabilized the predator when it pinned small prey to the group – just like some modern birds of prey do today.

Psittacosaurus

Feathers were thought to have evolved in birds and other extinct theropods. However, the discovery of long quills sprouting from the top of the tail of this Jehol ornithischian suggests feathers may be much older and widespread than previously thought.

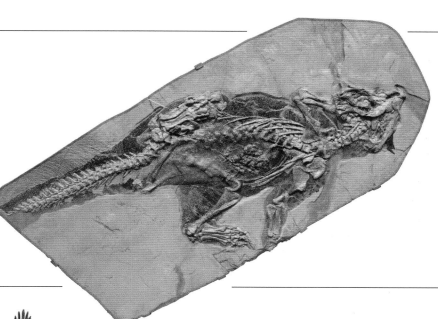

Incisivosaurus

The Chinese fossils never cease to amaze – but nobody expected to find a goofy dinosaur with big front teeth! *Incisivosaurus*, named in 2002, is a relative of *Oviraptor* (see p.135) and a member of a group of usually toothless theropods. The teeth were not sharp, so perhaps this strange-looking dinosaur was a herbivore. It could have used its front teeth to snatch up tough plant stems.

Dinosaur appearance

An increasing number of discoveries are revealing information about dinosaurs' soft tissues, such as skin. Imprints reveal scaly, bumpy skin, whilst fossilized skin and feathers are known in exquisite detail thanks to high-tech analyses.

Some very special fossils even preserve pigments, helping to unlock the colours of the creature. Camouflage patterns have been seen in some, whilst display patterns are known from the feathers of others.

Shiny feathers

The preserved pigments in the feathers of the tiny *Microraptor* showed their feathers were shiny, reflecting light to create colour. Comparing these pigments with those of modern birds have shown how these were like the feathers of starlings (left), for example, and may have had an important role in display.

Shedding skin

A study of the fossilized skin fragments, revealed some close dinosaurs relatives of birds, including *Beipiaosaurus* (right) and *Confuciusornis* (see p.116), shed their skin in small flakes and not in pieces or as a whole, like modern day snakes.

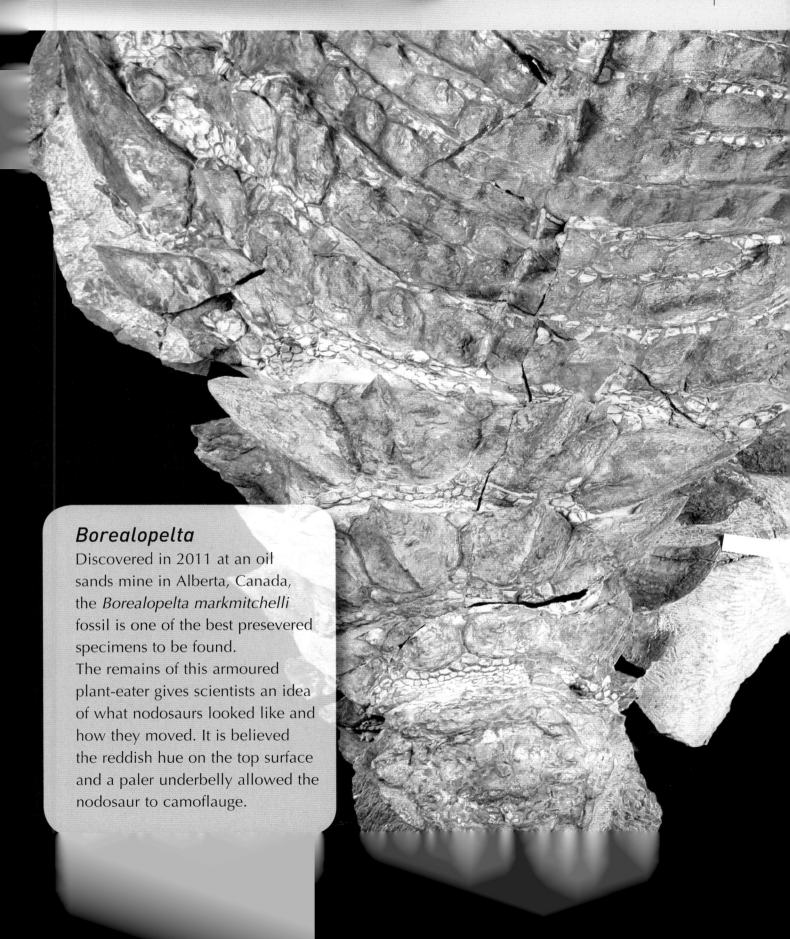

Borealopelta

Discovered in 2011 at an oil sands mine in Alberta, Canada, the *Borealopelta markmitchelli* fossil is one of the best presevered specimens to be found.

The remains of this armoured plant-eater gives scientists an idea of what nodosaurs looked like and how they moved. It is believed the reddish hue on the top surface and a paler underbelly allowed the nodosaur to camoflauge.

MICRORAPTOR

IN 2000, AN ASTONISHING FOUR-WINGED DINOSAUR FROM CHINA WAS UNVEILED. *MICRORAPTOR* POSSESSED LONG FEATHERS ON BOTH ITS ARMS AND LEGS. WHETHER IT COULD FLY AND HOW IT MOVED IN THE AIR HAS BEEN A SOURCE OF INTERESTING RESEARCH AND EXPERIMENTATION.

FOSSIL FINDS

Like much of the Jehol Biota, many of the fossils are exquisitely preserved. Several species have been named, although more recent research suggests these are all the same animal, and the differences in their anatomy is the result of natural variation within a population.

JINGMAI O'CONNOR

Jingmai O'Connor is an expert in the evolution of flight and the dinosaur-bird transition. Some of her recent work has explored the diet and digestion of *Microraptor*. She helped name a new species of lizard found inside the stomach of one *Microraptor* (right), and showed that this dinosaur couldn't throw up pellets of undigested food, like some modern birds.

IN THE FOREST

Microraptor is a dromaeosaurid dinosaur and not a bird and how it moved in the air has long been debated. Initially thought as a glider, some recent work has suggested the wings were big enough to generate lift and that it was capable of flapping. It is likely that this topic will be revisited in the future.

The Chinese birds

Until more recently, there was a long gap between the discovery of the first bird, *Archaeopteryx* (pp.84–5), and those of the Cretaceous.

The remarkable diversity of the Jehol Biota helped bridge this gap with the discovery of new fossil birds, revealing new lineages and helping chart the evolution of certain behaviours.

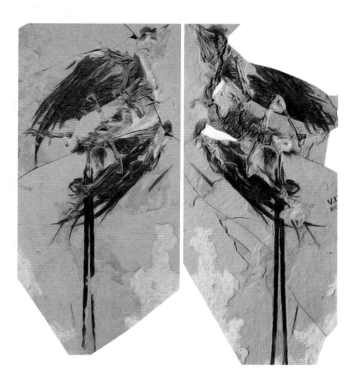

Eoconfuciusornis

One of the oldest confuciusornids (an extinct bird group close to modern forms), *Eoconfuciusornis* was named in 2008. The original specimen (above), is a thin slab of rock split in two. In some specimens, soft tissues like the wing membranes have been preserved and have helped study any flying capabilities.

Confuciusornis

Named after the great Chinese philosopher Confucius, this is one of the most common Early Cretaceous birds – several hundred complete specimens have been reported. Compared to the short tails of females, males possessed a pair of additional streamer-like feathers that were likely for display.

Longipteryx

This small bird was unusual in that it had a long beak, with a group of small teeth at the tip. *Longipteryx* may have been a diving bird that plunged into lakes and rivers, snapping up fishes or small shrimps.

Sapeornis

Sapeornis was a medium-sized Jehol bird that perched in trees. The fossils show a short, bony stump for a tail skeleton, as in modern birds. One specimen has rounded pieces of grit in its stomach that it may have swallowed for grinding up plant food.

Jeholornis

This relatively large bird was about the size of a turkey. Perhaps, like turkeys and chickens, it ran about on the ground, and only flew when it needed to escape from a predator. The tail feathers probably had a role in display.

EARTH EVIDENCE

SMALL EGGS

The Jehol bird specimens are amazing and many thousands have been found since 1995. Some, like this fossil of two *Confuciusornis* (left), contain two skeletons – the drawing on the right shows them clearly. The preserved detail has allowed scientists to better understand their lives. One recent study, for instance, argues early birds like *Confuciusornis* were too heavy to sit on the eggs, unlike their modern day cousins.

Psittacosaurus

Psittacosaurus was a common little herbivore and distant relative of its more famous ceratopsian cousins, such as *Triceratops*.

Unlike later ceratopsians *Psittacosaurus* lacked elaborate frills and elongated horns, although some species did have impressive cheek horns.

Fossil nest?

The discovery of over 20 small *Psittacosaurus* babies alongside the remains of a larger specimen appeared to show parental care in this dinosaur. However, the larger specimen was later shown to be a juvenile, around five years old. *Psittacosaurus* couldn't breed until ten years old, so what was going on with this group of herbivores?

Modelling the 'nest'

The discovery appears to show some form of cooperation between differently aged juveniles. Juvenile cooperation may have helped ensure survival of young individuals during the dangerous Early Cretaceous.

Growing up

Psittacosaurus underwent what is known as a 'postural shift' as it matured. Young scurried about on four legs, but as they grew older, they became bipedal. This change is seen in the limb proportions and also in the brain structure.

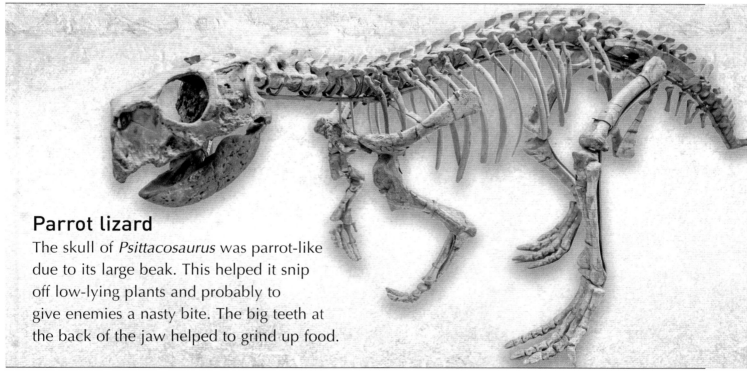

Parrot lizard

The skull of *Psittacosaurus* was parrot-like due to its large beak. This helped it snip off low-lying plants and probably to give enemies a nasty bite. The big teeth at the back of the jaw helped to grind up food.

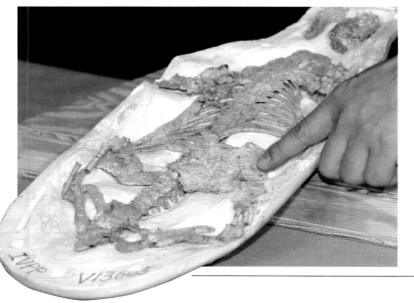

Bottom of the food chain

Psittacosaurus was small and needed camouflage to hide from predators. Fossilised pigments show it had a brown back and pale underbelly, a form of camouflage known as countershading. Hatchlings and babies were very vulnerable, and some have been found inside the ribcage of a Cretaceous mammal, *Repanomamus*.

The Cloverly Formation

Deposited in an ancient floodplain environment, the rocks of the Cloverly Formation contain a rich crop of Early Cretaceous dinosaurs.

John Ostrom and his team had heard of bones in the Cloverly Formation, and they set up field camps. In 1964, they found skeletons of *Deinonychus*, an efficient theropod hunter.

Deinonychus

Over the course of a few years, Ostrom's expeditions uncovered the remains of several dromaeosaurid individuals, which he later named *Deinonychus* or 'terrible claw'. With so much material, Ostrom was able to describe this predator in great detail.

Terrible claw

Like many of its cousins, *Deinonychus* had an enlarged claw on each foot, which was held off the ground. It would then be slashed down with some force.

The large slashing claw on the back feet would sweep downwards, doing enormous damage to prey.

Deinonychus and birds

Ostrom's work on *Deinonychus* showed dromaeosaurids were close relatives of birds. Ostrom also showed the similarities between *Deinonychus* and the first bird, *Archaeopteryx* (see pp.84–5).

Hunting as a pack?

In 1995, Ostrom reported a new excavation site where a dead *Tenontosaurus* (above) was surrounded by some dead *Deinonychus*. He guessed that this smart predator hunted in packs. However, this is very sophisticated behaviour and probably did not occur in theropods. Analysis of the feet show that the claw was adapted for pinning down smaller prey, not attacking large herbivores.

The Bighorn Basin

Many dinosaur sites in North America are in 'badlands', so called because they are 'bad lands' for farming and people. But these open, desert-like areas are 'good lands' for dinosaurs – palaeontologists can spot bones in the rapidly eroding gullies. The Bighorn Basin, Wyoming, is 130km across and includes the Cloverly Formation.

John Ostrom

Professor of palaeontology at Yale University, John Ostrom (1928–2005) worked first on hadrosaurs, and then began excavations in the Cloverly Formation. His discovery of *Deinonychus* led to a complete revolution in modern palaeontological thought. He rekindled the debate that birds evolved from dinosaurs, and that many, including *Deinonychus*, were possibly warm blooded.

ELRHAZ FORMATION

THE ELRHAZ FORMATION OF NIGER, IN WEST AFRICA, CONTAINS ONE OF THE BEAST EARLY CRETACEOUS FAUNAS IN THE WORLD.

OURANOSAURUS

Herds of this large ornithopod once roamed the floodplains of Niger, in North Africa. Like many of its cousins, including *Iguanodon* (pp.100–01), it bore a small thumb spike on each hand. The large sail along its back remains a mystery, but such strange structures usually have a role in display.

Nigersaurus had the most teeth of any sauropod, with hundreds of active and replacement teeth packed into what is known as a 'dental battery'.

NIGERSAURUS

This unusual, shovel-mouthed sauropod was a low-browsing specialist. The tips of its jaws were expanded, allowing it to crop large mouthfuls of plants. At about 9m long, is short neck meant it couldn't reach high into the canopy, and likely favoured low-lying plants.

SARCOSUCHUS

One of the largest crocodilian relatives to have walked the Earth, *Sarcosuchus* weighed about 2 tonnes and was up to 8m in length, with a skull as big as a human adult's body. It prowled the river banks, crushing fish and larger prey – such as *Ouranosaurus* – with the 132 teeth in its fearsome jaws.

The crested spinosaurs

The spinosaurs were a group of dinosaurs that appeared in the Early Cretaceous. The name refers to the long spines on their backs.

The group most likely arose in the Jurassic, however nothing bar a few teeth is known about these primitive forms. The Cretaceous spinosaurs are mainly known from partial skeletons.

Baryonyx

A partial spinosaur skeleton was found in England, which helped palaeontologists to understand the group better. *Baryonyx* had spines down its back and a long-snouted, crocodile-like skull. The remains of fish and juvenile dinosaurs were found in its ribcage, suggesting a mixed diet.

Ernst Stromer

Ernst Stromer (1870–1952) found the first spinosaur, *Spinosaurus*, in Egypt, and named it in 1915. He brought this and many other dinosaurs back to Munich in Germany. Sadly, the museum was bombed in 1944, and the entire collection was lost, apart from his journals and the published description and drawings of *Spinosaurus*.

Suchomimus

In 1998, Paul Sereno and his team found *Suchomimus*, 'crocodile mimic', in Niger, just south of the Sahara desert. This 11m-long African spinosaur was very like *Baryonyx*. It had the same crocodile-like skull.

Assembling a skeleton
Paul Sereno puts the finishing touches to a museum mount of his discovery, *Suchomimus*. This new find is a good example of the anatomy of spinosaurs. In life, the long spines down the backbone supported a low crest – the spines were longer and the crest higher in *Spinosaurus*.

Polar dinosaurs

During the Cretaceous, the South Pole was unlike today and was covered in lush forests supported a rich fauna.

In the Cretaceous, Australia lay closer to the South Pole. South Australia, where dinosaurs have been found, was in icy cold latitudes.

Dinosaur Cove

One site in Victoria, on the south coast of Australia, has produced many dinosaur bones and is called Dinosaur Cove. The rocks are Early Cretaceous, from about 106 mya, younger than the Jehol Group of China (see pp.106–7) and the Cloverly Formation of North America (see pp.120–1).

In the field

Dinosaur Cove was a tough place to work. The bones were buried in hard rock that had to be drilled out, so the team dug caves into the cliffs. They even had to use explosives.

Leaellynasaura and *Timimus* wander along beside the lake in Dinosaur Cove.

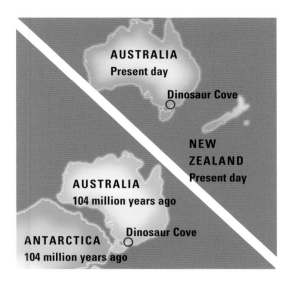

Near the pole

This geographic reconstruction shows that, during the Cretaceous, Australia was breaking free from Antarctica as Gondwana broke up. Parts of Australia lay within the Antarctic circle, and Dinosaur Cove was close to the south pole. Lakes and rivers would have frozen in winter.

Atlascopcosaurus

This small plant-eater is a relative of *Iguanadon* from England (see pp.102–3). *Atlascopcosaurus* was 2–3m long, but it is known only from a few fragments of the skull and skeleton, so this reconstruction is based on its close relatives.

Timimus

There are not many large predators in the Dinosaur Cove deposits. Some isolated leg bones show that *Timimus* may have been a tyrannosauroid, a member of a group that began in the Jurassic.

Leaellynasaura

This small herbivore is named after Leaellyn, the daughter of Tom and Patricia Vickers-Rich, who discovered it. *Leaellynasaura* was less than 1m long and fed on the ferns and cycads found at the same site.

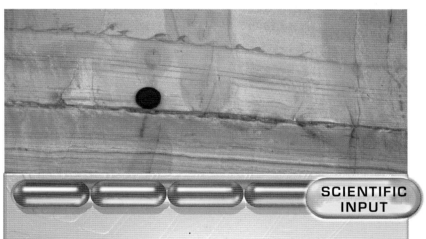

SCIENTIFIC INPUT

HARSH TIMES

This vertical section of finely-banded mud has 'flame structures', where the damp mud was frozen in winter, and then melted and became fluid. The little dinosaurs of Dinosaur Cove would have been subjected to long periods of darkness and freezing temperatures in the winter, meaning food was hard to come by. It's suggested some of the smaller forms lived in burrows.

Dinosaur facts

The world of the dinosaurs was full of many plants and animals that no longer exist because they have become extinct. However, there were many other plants and animals that lived during the Mesozoic that we would find familiar today.

PLANTS
- Mosses – low green moss covered the rocks and trees.
- Ferns – fern fronds filled dark nooks and crannies.
- Tree ferns – dinosaurs loved to eat tree ferns, but they are not as common today.
- Conifer trees – many dinosaurs fed on the needles and broader leaves of ancestors of the pines and the monkey puzzle.
- Flowering plants – dinosaurs did not eat grass, cabbages or flowers, but the first flowering plants, such as magnolia, appeared in the middle of the Cretaceous.

ANIMALS
- Worms – earthworms churned the soil.
- Snails – slugs and snails lived among the dead leaves and fed on plants.
- Beetles – bugs, cockroaches and beetles lived on trees and under leaves.
- Ants and termites – in the Cretaceous, these colony-living insects appeared after the evolution of flowering plants.
- Bees and wasps – these honey-gatherers appeared in the Cretaceous.
- Butterflies and moths – these insects fed on nectar from Cretaceous flowers.
- Fishes – modern-style fishes lived in the sea, and in rivers and lakes.
- Frogs and salamanders – these amphibians appeared in the Triassic, becoming common in the Cretaceous.
- Lizards – the first lizards are Jurassic, and many modern groups appeared in the Cretaceous.
- Snakes – the first snakes appeared in the Cretaceous.
- Turtles – these animals swam in ponds and crept about on the land from the Late Triassic onwards.
- Crocodiles – these fish-eaters lived in ponds and seas from the Jurassic.
- Birds – *Archaeopteryx* appeared in the Late Jurassic and birds became very varied in the Cretaceous.
- Mammals – the first mammals of the Triassic gave rise to some modern-style mammals in the Cretaceous.

The fossil skeleton of a *Dromaeosaur* about to attack its prey

WEBSITES ON LIFE DURING THE MESOZOIC ERA

www.ucmp.berkeley.edu/mesozoic/mesozoic.html   A guide to the main groups of life in the Mesozoic.

www.livescience.com/38596-mesozoic-era.html   An in-depth look at climate and life in the Mesozoic.

http://palaeo.gly.bris.ac.uk/macro/supertree/KTR.html   How flora and fauna changed in the Cretaceous.

www.fossilmuseum.net/Paleobiology/Mesozoic_Paleobiology.htm   Lots of Mesozoic fossils.

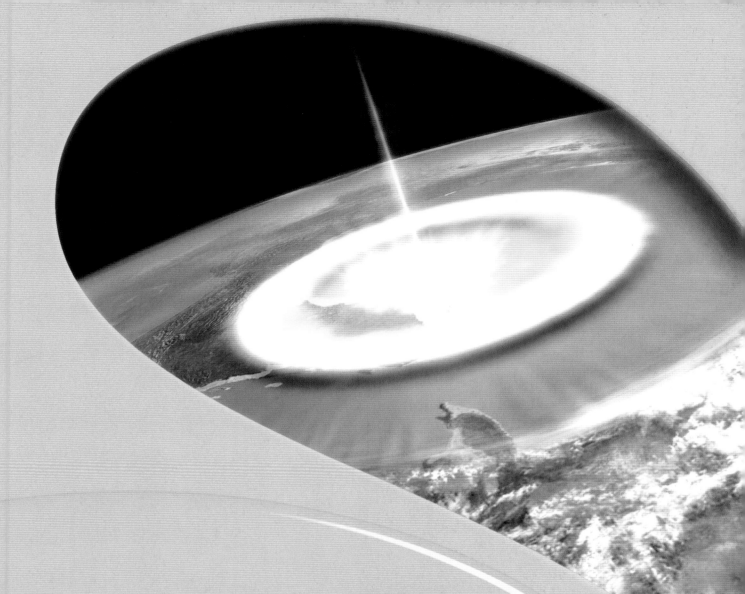

CHANGE AND EXTINCTION

The Late Cretaceous saw the continents continue to move apart. Dinosaurs in different parts of the world evolved to become different from each other. New groups, such as hadrosaurs, ceratopsians and ankylosaurs became common. But it all ended 66 million years ago when a massive asteroid hit the Earth, killing the non-bird dinosaurs and many other forms of life.

Mongolian expeditions

When the first fossils were found in Mongolia, northern China, in the 1920s, they caused a sensation.

The first expedition was from New York City in search of early human fossils. Instead, they found an amazing haul of dinosaur skeletons.

Roy Chapman Andrews

Chapman Andrews (1884–1960) was hired by the American Museum of Natural History to lead the expeditions to Mongolia. He had already toured the world, including China, collecting specimens for the museum, and he was used to the difficult conditions he would meet in the desert.

Fossil bonanza

The Mongolian expeditions were fruitful, with many famous specimens discovered including *Psittacosaurus* and *Protoceratops* (see pp. 118–9), as well as odd theropod *Oviraptor*. Nests were also uncovered, which caused quite a stir.

The sands of the Gobi Desert are a hostile environment in which to hunt for dinosaurs.

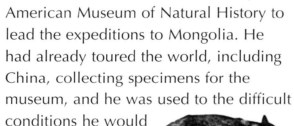

Velociraptor

Another of the 1923 finds was *Velociraptor*, an extraordinary little theropod. Its name means 'speedy hunter'. This 1m-long predator is now known to be a close relative of *Deinonychus* (see p.121).

Velociraptor's skull

The narrow, lightweight skull had small yet serrated teeth. *Velociraptor* probably pinned down prey with its feet before clamping with its jaws.

Members of the 1925 expedition push their vehicles through the sand.

Fossil sites

Mongolia

During the Cretaceous, Mongolia was similar to today – arid and hot, but cold in some areas. There was little water apart from a few oases and short-lived streams.

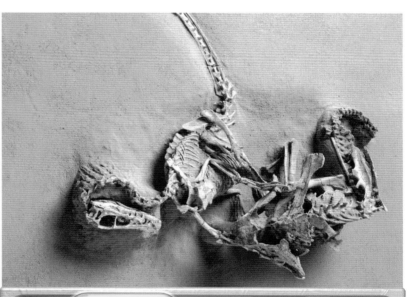

AMAZING FACTS

FIGHT TO THE DEATH

This amazing fossil, discovered in 1971, is of a *Velociraptor* (left) attacking a *Protoceratops* (right), which bit down on the predator's right hand with its beak-like jaws. *Velociraptor*'s hind claw is embedded in the throat area of the *Protoceratops*. Palaeontologists have debated how this fight scene was preserved. The struggling dinosaurs may have been overcome by a sandstorm that killed them instantly.

The Nemegt Formation

The Nemegt Formation is the source of diverse dinosaur fauna, including the pachycephalosaur *Homalocephale*, the sauropod *Nemegtosaurus* and the theropod *Tarbosaurus*.

The formation was discovered by US expeditions in the 1920s, but it was excavated thoroughly by expeditions from the Soviet Union in the 1950s. The Soviets used bulldozers to excavate skeletons of the giant theropod *Tarbosaurus* (see pp.134–5). Expeditions from Poland in the 1960s unearthed *Nemegtosaurus*.

Fossil finds

A Mongolian boy proudly holds up the thigh bone of *Nemegtosaurus*, the sauropod. Many of the fossils from Mongolia are in excellent condition, and complete, like this specimen. Since 1960, palaeontologists have trained in Mongolia, and much of the work is done by these scientists, working with overseas collaborators from the USA, Japan and Europe.

The first task is to protect the fossil bones with a covering of paper or foil.

Plaster powder is mixed with water to make a paste, which is smeared on to bandages.

The bandages of sacking, or burlap, in plaster are smoothed over the bones.

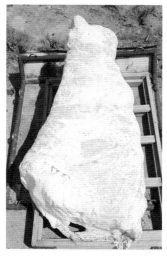

The bandaged block is allowed to dry, and then is turned over. Wooden planks are plastered onto the base to strengthen the block.

Excavating fossil bones

Dinosaur bones may seem big and tough, but they are actually fragile. Since the early days, palaeontologists have used bandages in plaster to strengthen the specimens – the process is the same as when doctors bandage a broken leg. The plaster protects the bones while they are in transit. It is cut off in the lab and the bones can then be carefully removed from the rock.

Nemegt expedition

A line of 11 trucks sets out across the wild plains of Mongolia to excavate giant dinosaurs in the Nemegt Formation. Expeditions to such remote areas often have to be large – the palaeontologists must carry all their equipment with them, including enough food, water and fuel for a month or more.

Theropods of Mongolia

Various expeditions revealed a huge range of Late Cretaceous theropods from several different formations.

Some were herbivorous, whilst others sat at the top of the food chain.

Gallimimus

This ornithomimid belonged to one of several theropod groups that lost their teeth. It had a sharp-edged beak to eat plants. At one time, people thought that ornithomimids were egg-eaters.

Saurornithoides

The troodontids were slender and fast-moving dinosaurs. *Saurornithoides* was less than 2m long and almost certainly covered in feathers. It had good eyesight and a large brain, probably to help it hunt fast-moving lizards and mammals.

Saurornithoides had long-fingered hands for snatching prey.

Tarbosaurus' skull

This skull was fairly broad, particularly at the back, which allowed plenty of space for the jaw closing muscles.

The massive hindlimbs had large, three-toed feet for holding down the prey.

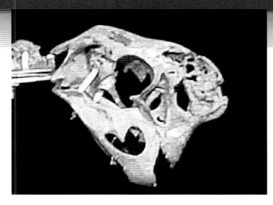

Citipati's skull

One of the weirdest toothless theropods was *Citiati*, with its high, short snout. The skull is very lightweight, with enormous openings and thin, bony struts. Its distinctive crest was likely for display.

Citipati

This is one of the astonishing dinosaurs discovered during the US expeditions to Mongolia in the 1920s (see pp.130–1). Several specimens have famously been found sitting on top of nests.

Citipati was likely covered in feathers.

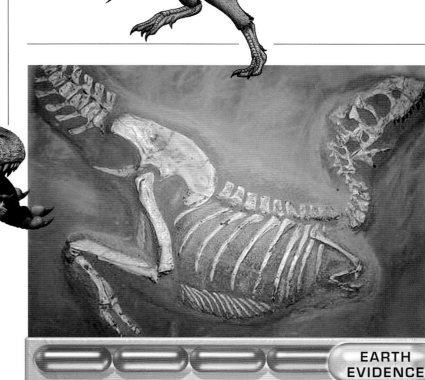

Tarbosaurus

The first skeletons of *Tarbosaurus* were excavated in the 1950s, in the Nemegt Formation (see pp.132–3). The dinosaur was a close relative of *Tyrannosaurus* from North America (see pp.144–5), but there are differences in the skull.

EARTH EVIDENCE

PERFECT FOSSILS

Various growth stages of *Tarbosaurus* have been found, although they were initially thought to belong to different theropods. The Soviet palaeontologists had to drive massive trucks and bulldozers to the Nemegt, and they even used explosives to speed up the process of extracting the fossil skeletons. These were transported back to Russia by truck and train, and they may now be seen on show in Moscow.

THERIZINOSAURS

Therizinosaurs were an enigmatic group of herbivorous theropods, whose remains initially confused palaeontologists. With more finds across the Northern Hemisphere, scientists now have a much better understanding of this group of dinosaurs.

THERIZINOSAURUS

When Soviet palaeontologists dug up a number of massive, 1m-long scythe-like claws, they thought that these came from a giant turtle. The dinosaur was named by Evgeny Maleev in 1954 and other bones came to light in the following years. However, it wasn't until the 1970s that *Therizinosaurus* was acknowledged to be a dinosaur. The group to which it belonged was still poorly understood, and it took decades and several skeletons of its cousins for their relationship with advanced theropods to be clarified.

GIANT CLAWS

Therizinosaurus means 'scythe lizard' and looking at its huge claws, it's easy to understand why. Three claws were on each front limb and measured nearly 1m in length. They may have been used to pull food towards the *Therizinosaurus'* mouth. Their large size may have been used to scare off predators, but this idea is still to be proved.

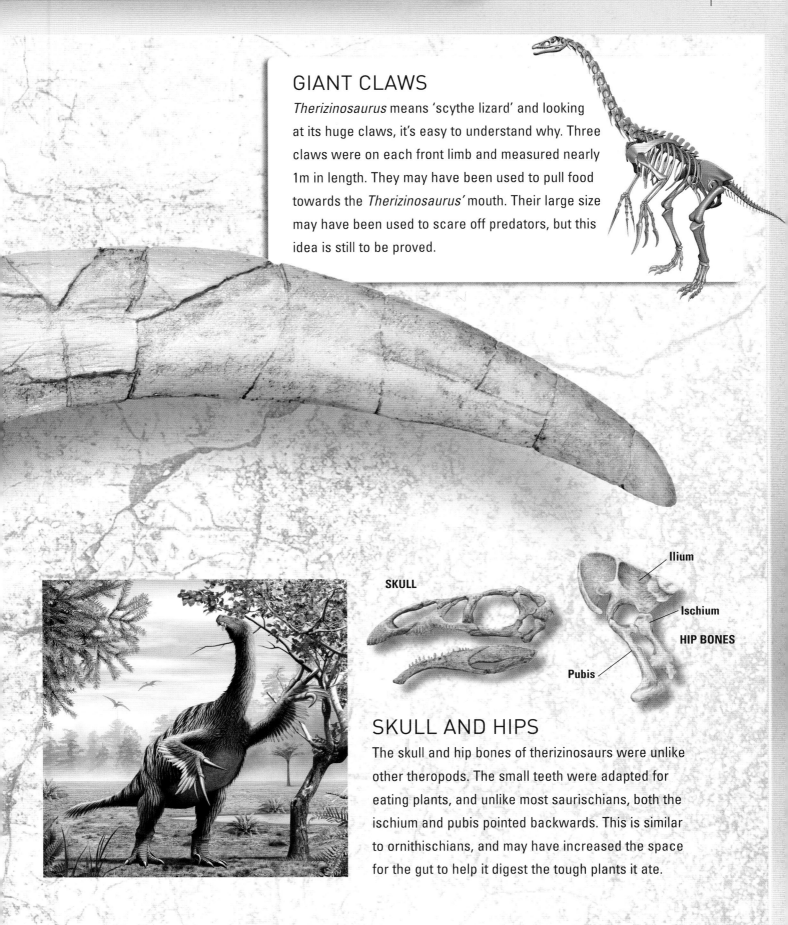

SKULL

Ilium

Ischium

HIP BONES

Pubis

SKULL AND HIPS

The skull and hip bones of therizinosaurs were unlike other theropods. The small teeth were adapted for eating plants, and unlike most saurischians, both the ischium and pubis pointed backwards. This is similar to ornithischians, and may have increased the space for the gut to help it digest the tough plants it ate.

Hadrosaurs

In the Late Cretaceous, some of the most common dinosaurs were the hadrosaurs, close relatives of ornithopods such as *Iguanodon* (see pp.100–1).

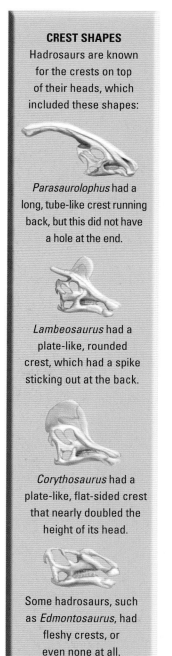

CREST SHAPES
Hadrosaurs are known for the crests on top of their heads, which included these shapes:

Parasaurolophus had a long, tube-like crest running back, but this did not have a hole at the end.

Lambeosaurus had a plate-like, rounded crest, which had a spike sticking out at the back.

Corythosaurus had a plate-like, flat-sided crest that nearly doubled the height of its head.

Some hadrosaurs, such as *Edmontosaurus*, had fleshy crests, or even none at all.

Hadrosaurs were extremely successful, and a key adaptation was the evolution of dental batteries, which helped them grind down plants.

Anatomy

Except for the head, the general hadrosaur shape was relatively similar across most the group. They typically moved on all four legs, with the hand modified to help bare weight. Some hadrosaurs evolved large, showy crests, whilst others developed pronounced snouts.

Hadrosaurs moved on all four legs, but may have reared up from time to time.

Making sounds

When palaeontologists looked inside the crests of some hadrosaurs, such as *Parasaurolophus*, they found the nostrils ran up inside the crests. The complex airways acted as resonance chambers, helping the dinosaur communicate. Different crest shapes likely produced different hooting and honking sounds.

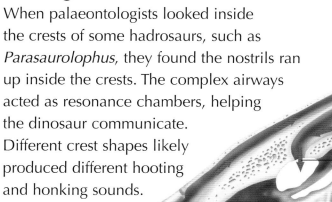

Air travels through the head and up nostril.

Air would pass into the lungs through here

CHANGE AND EXTINCTION | **139**

Living in a herd

Many hadrosaur fossils have been found in large numbers, sometimes dozens of skeletons in one site. These 'assemblages' suggest that the hadrosaurs lived in herds. Great herds of hadrosaurs, even several species together, may have fed peacefully side by side, not unlike herds of antelope in Africa today.

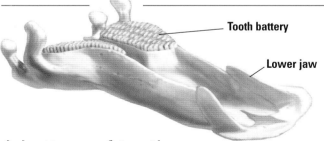

Tooth battery

Lower jaw

A battery of teeth

Some hadrosaurs had 2,000 teeth arranged in rows at the back of the jaw. Unlike most vertebrates, their teeth never fell out, and instead formed a large grinding platform with which to break down plants and extract as much nutrients as possible.

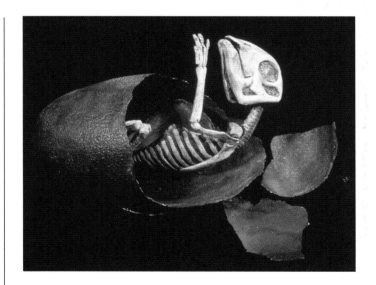

Hatching out

Some hadrosaur eggs have been found with unhatched babies inside. At time of hatching, the eggs weighed around 1 kg. This model shows that, just before hatching, this baby hadrosaur filled the egg, with its tail wrapped round its body. The baby had a short skull and huge eyes.

The Romanian islands

Late Cretaceous dinosaurs are rare in parts of Europe because most of the continent was under ocean.

However, there were some islands in the south of France and Spain, and in eastern Europe, where Romania is today. Some very strange little dinosaurs have been found in these areas.

Hateg Island

The Hateg area of modern Romania was the setting for the famous novel Dracula, however back in the very latest Cretaceous it was a small island teaming with prehistoric life. Today, the area is a dinosaur geopark.

Magyarosaurus

This sauropod was named in 1932, and was only 6m in length – small compared to the closely related titanosaurs, which were 12m or longer. Palaeontologists realized this was a 'dwarf species' – it was smaller than its relatives because it lived on an island.

Hatzegopteryx

The apex predator on Hateg Island may not have been a theropod, but a huge pterosaur with a wingspan of over 10m. Its neck bones were bulkier than its close cousins, with a wider than usual skull. This giant may have stalked the dwarf dinosaurs in a manner similar to some modern-day storks and hornbills, preying on juveniles.

Balaur

Named after a Romanian dragon, this theropod was unique in possessing two killer claws on each foot. Palaeontologists initially thought it was a dromaeosaurid, however subsequent analyses showed it was a bizarre form more closely related to modern birds.

Baron Franz Nopcsa

Franz Nopcsa (1877–1933) was born of a noble family on the borders of Romania and Hungary. He found fossils on his family estates at Hateg, and named many of the dinosaurs, realizing that they were 'island dwarfs'.

Struthiosaurus

This Hateg dinosaur is an ankylosaur, up to 2.5m long. *Struthiosaurus* is known from several European islands, in Romania, Austria and France, and it seems to have been more like the Early Cretaceous ankylosaurs from elsewhere.

The small ankylosaur browsed on low-lying vegetation.

Argentinian finds

The Late Cretaceous of Argentina was home to a diverse fauna that included gigantic sauropods and bizarre little theropods. Large killers prowled the top of the food chain.

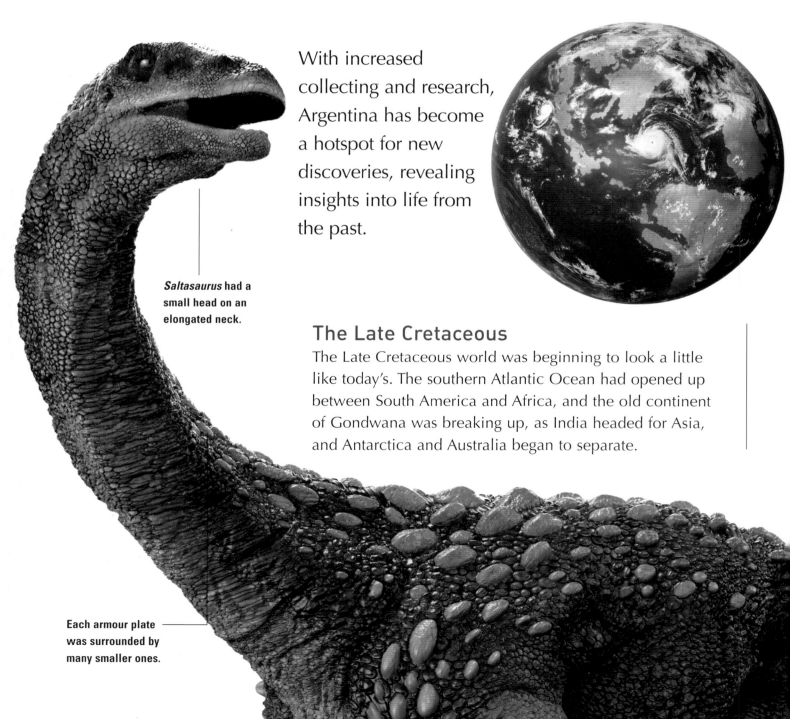

With increased collecting and research, Argentina has become a hotspot for new discoveries, revealing insights into life from the past.

Saltasaurus had a small head on an elongated neck.

Each armour plate was surrounded by many smaller ones.

The Late Cretaceous

The Late Cretaceous world was beginning to look a little like today's. The southern Atlantic Ocean had opened up between South America and Africa, and the old continent of Gondwana was breaking up, as India headed for Asia, and Antarctica and Australia began to separate.

Titanosaur nest site

Several thousand eggs, nests and even embryos were found in Argentina, revealing a sauropod hatchery. Called Auca Maheuvo, this site revealed a type of titanosaur repeatedly came to the same place to lay eggs in shallow, bowl-like nests in the ground. They probably didn't look after their young.

Alvarezsaurus

This small theropod was named in 1991 on the basis of an incomplete skeleton. About 1m long, the animal was slender and lightweight. Its small and stout forelimbs may have been adapted to dig termite mounds.

Saltasaurus

One group of sauropods, the titanosaurs, remained important herbivores in the Late Cretaceous ecosystems of South America. *Saltasaurus* (left) was around 12m long, which is relatively small compared to some of its cousins, and had bony scutes in its skin. Scutes were present in other titanosaurs. Youngsters may have been used them for defence, and adults as a mineral store for egg building.

Abelisaurus

A great predator of the Argentinian Late Cretaceous was *Abelisaurus*. It was up to 9m long, similar in size to many tyrannosaurs. But *Abelisaurus* belongs to a more ancient primitive theropod group, with short skulls and often with crests above the eyes. These abelisaurids also lived in India and Africa, as well as Madagascar.

TYRANNOSAURIDS

THE MOST FEARSOME AND FAMOUS DINOSAURS ARE THE TYRANNOSAURIDS. THESE HUGE HUNTERS, INCLUDING THE 9-TONNE *TYRANNOSAURUS REX*, WERE THE TOP PREDATORS THROUGHOUT THE NORTHERN HEMISPHERE IN THE LATE CRETACEOUS.

TYRANNOSAURUS REX

The largest of the tyrannosaurs, *Tyrannosaurus rex*, reached lengths of over 12m and weighed around 9 tonnes. With a bite force of 4 tonnes, its teeth could drive through flesh and crush bone. Although not the fastest of dinosaurs, it was a formidable predator with good eyesight and sense of smell, capable of taking down big opponents.

Tyrannosaurus had a bite force of over 4 tonnes.

CURVED TEETH

Tyrannosaurids had a typical theropod body shape, but differed in several aspects. For instance, their teeth (right) were much thicker, helping them crush through bone. Other theropods teeth were more daggerlike. Tyrannosaurids snout bones were also fused together to help cope with the stress of biting hard.

ASIAN TYRANNOSAURS

Some evidence suggests that
Tyrannosaurus was a migrant
from Asia, crossing an
ancient land bridge
that linked Asia
to Alaska.
However, more
research is needed
to better understand
this claim. It was closely
related to Asian tyrannosaurs
like *Tarbosaurus* (see pp.134–5)

Triceratops

The ceratopsids were plant-eating dinosaurs of the Late Cretaceous. Their massive heads bore spikes and horns, along with a large frill.

MAKING A POINT
Ceratopsid skulls were mainly adapted to attract mates.

Triceratops had a broad frill, a horn on the nose, and one over each eye socket.

Chasmosaurus also had three horns, but it also had a square-topped neck frill.

Centrosaurus had a huge nose horn, and small horns on the back edge of the frill.

Pachyrhinosaurus had spikes on its frill, as well as a blunt boss on its nose.

Triceratops, the best-known ceratopsid, was one of the last to appear before the Mesozoic ended.

Weapons for fighting
The three-horned face of *Triceratops* may have been adapted to fighting one another. Battle marks on fossil frills show the large brow horns may have locked together during tussles, perhaps to claim mating rights.

Solitary beast?
Other ceratopsids probably lived in herds, however *Triceratops* remains are often found on their own, suggesting that these were solitary herbivores. However, the discovery of a group of three young individuals may mean *Triceratops* were more social than once thought.

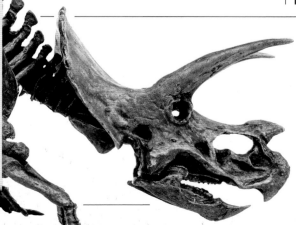

Solid frill
The neck frill was formed of expanded bones that made up the back of the skull. To support the mass of the head, the first three vertebrae of *Triceratops* were fused together for strength.

Elephant size

At over 8m in length and weighing around 9 tonnes, *Triceratops* was a formidable animal. Similar to the hadrosaurs (pp.138–9), *Triceratops* and its cousins had a battery of teeth to help grind plant material that it cropped with their parrot-like beaks.

The last dinosaurs

Once it was thought the number of non-bird dinosaurs was in decline at the end of the Late Cretaceous.

However, new research has shown dinosaurs were diverse and abundant right to the end. There is no sign that their days were numbered, and this suggests they were killed by something out of the ordinary.

Edmontosaurus

Many hadrosaurs lived right at the end of the Cretaceous, two species of *Edmontosaurus* among them. This 13m-long dinosaur was one of the largest hadrosaurs, and it is known especially from Canada (it is named after Edmonton, the capital of Alberta).

Hell Creek

The Hell Creek Formation is one of the best-known Late Cretaceous rock units that yields dinosaurs. The rich fossil beds were discovered in the late nineteenth century and it is across several US states – North Dakota, South Dakota, Montana, Colorado and Wyoming. The rocks were laid down in ancient rivers towards the end of the Cretaceous.

Pachycephalosaurus

This mid-sized dinosaur was a relative of *Triceratops*, and sported a 25cm-thick dome on its head. Skull injuries reveal the dome was probably used to fight and ram others over resources.

Ankylosaurus

One of the largest of the armoured dinosaurs, *Ankylosaurus* was 10m or more in length, and armed with a great, bony club on its tail. Its whole body was encased in tough bony scutes and it may have even had a bony eyelid to protect each eye!

Anzu

This large oviraptorosaur would have been covered in feathers in life. It may have taken up a 'generalist' role in their ecosystem, eating a range of plants and animals.

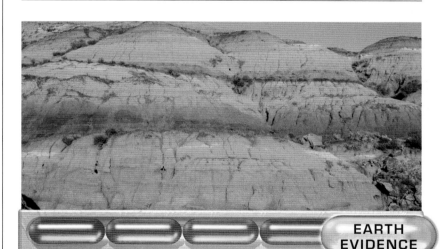

EARTH EVIDENCE

THE K-Pg BOUNDARY

A thin line of sediment separates the Late Cretaceous rocks from the Tertiary rocks above. This line can be found across the globe and marks the extinction event at the end of the Mesozoic. All the non-bird dinosaurs are found below that line, but some other animals made it past the boundary, including birds, mammals and crocodilians. The abbreviation K-Pg means Cretaceous–Palaeocene.

IMPACT!

FOR YEARS, SCIENTISTS HAVE DEBATED THE END OF THE DINOSAURS 66 MYA. SEA REPTILES, PTEROSAURS, AMMONITES, BELEMNITES AND MANY OTHER CREATURES BECAME EXTINCT AT EXACTLY THE SAME TIME. MANY THEORIES HAVE BEEN TESTED AND REJECTED. THE CURRENT PREFERRED THEORY, SUPPORTED BY A HUGE AMOUNT OF EVIDENCE, IS THAT THE EARTH WAS HIT BY A MASSIVE ASTEROID.

HOW THE WORLD CHANGED

Upon impact, the asteroid was instantly destroyed and the rocks it crashed into tossed high into the air. The heat from the impact vaporized all surrounding life and wildfires burnt through forests. As it crashed into a shallow sea, mega tsunamis with waves several hundred metres high, devastated low-lying regions. The impact also sent fine dust and other chemicals into the atmosphere, almost blocking out the sun and causing the collapse of global food chains.

1. Large rocks and debris fly through the air on impact.

2. A tsunami hits the shore and churns beach rocks.

3. A hot shock wave through the air causes wildfire.

4. Fine dust descends from high in the atmosphere.

THE ASTEROID HITS

The meteorite was 10–15km across and it delivered an explosive force ten billion times more powerful than the largest ever atomic bomb. It punched deep into the Earth's crust and produced a huge crater. The force of the impact meant that the asteroid itself was reduced to dust – and this dust, together with millions of tonnes of rock, was thrown out of the crater.

Impact site

CHICXULUB CRATER

The 150km wide crater is found in the Gulf of Mexico, on the coastline near the town of Chicxulub after which it's named. Drilling into the crater site found a layer of jumbled rocks indicating a tsunami, whilst shocked quartz and melted rock preserve evidence of the force of the impact.

After the dinosaurs

When the dinosaurs had gone, the world must have seemed very empty. Gone were their huge bodies, the noise, mess and smell. But life carried on.

Insects, fishes, frogs, lizards, snakes, turtles, crocodiles, mammals and non-bird dinosaurs survived the K-Pg mass extinction. Mammals in particular began to populate the world.

Ptilodus

Ptilodus was around 30–50cm in size and survived the mass extinction. It may have had squirrel like behaviours and lived in trees, cutting and chewing its way through tough leaves and even wood.

The Palaeocene

The Palaeocene (66 to 56 mya) was the first time division of the Cenozoic. Mammals rapidly diversified in this time, whilst the surviving dinosaur group, birds, also radiated into new forms and lifestyles. Compared to the Mesozoic, the Palaeocene saw the overall climate start to cool.

Mammals

Mammals have hair, large brains, and they feed their young with milk. Mammals today include humans, monkeys, pigs, dogs, cats, mice, bats and whales. They have been successful because they can adapt to all habitats.

Chriacus

This 1m-long mammal probably fed on plants as well as insects and small mammals. It likely relied on its sense of smell more than vision, and could probably hear as well as a modern aardvark. It may be related to modern hoofed animals, but its relationships are uncertain.

Plesiadapis

This small, squirrel-like mammal appeared in the Late Palaeocene and may be related to modern primates, which includes monkeys and apes. Its skeleton indicates it was probably a good climber.

Cimolestes Many unusual mammals survived from the Cretaceous, including the cimolestids, but little is known about this sharp-toothed genus. They may have died out at the start of the Palaeocene and may be distantly related to some modern insect- or animal-eating mammals.

The Miocene and human origins

The Miocene was a key time in human evolution. In Africa, the great forests were filled with apes. By 15 mya, climates had become cooler and the forests smaller. Some apes, our ancestors, ventured out on the grassy plains and began to walk upright. Fossils of the oldest human relatives are 7–8 million years old, and *Australopithecus* (below) lived 4–1 mya. Modern humans arose in Africa about 200,000 years ago.

Evolution facts

The world has changed a great deal since the dinosaurs disappeared. Most of the modern birds and mammals, including humans, came on the scene in the last 66 million years. Here are some major steps in evolution after the dinosaurs.

- **66 mya** Beginning of the Palaeocene; the first primates – the order of mammals that includes monkeys, apes and humans – appear.
- **60–54 mya** First rodents and bats appear.
- **55 mya** The first monkeys and horses, appear.
- **50–35 mya** The first elephants, pigs, whales and songbirds appear.
- **40 mya** Grasses evolve from angiosperms and grassland spreads.
- **35 mya** Australia and South America separate from Antarctica; the first species of sabre-toothed cat, *Miomachairodus*, appears in Africa and Turkey.

- **35 mya** The largest land mammal ever appears – *Paraceratherium*, a giant rhinoceros of about 7.5m tall.
- **6 mya** The first in the human line, *Sahelanthropus* and *Orrorin*, appear in Africa.
- **4.8 mya** Mammoths appear in North America, Europe and Asia.
- **3 mya** South America re-joins North America at Panama, and their mammals mix.
- **2.5 mya** Beginning of the Pleistocene, the Great Ice Age with glacier ice spreading over a quarter of Earth's land surface; the woolly rhinoceros appears in Europe, North Africa and Asia.

- **1.8 mya** The first large-brained human, *Homo erectus*, appears in Africa.
- **300,000 years ago** The first members of our own species, *Homo sapiens*, appear in Africa.
- **100,000 years ago** The first modern humans appear in Asia and Europe.
- **32,000 years ago** Oldest known cave paintings are made in southern France.
- **18,000 years ago** Global warming begins, glacier ice begins to retreat and sea levels rise.
- **11,700 years ago** End of the Pleistocene and beginning of the Holocene (up to the present); the first humans appear in the Americas.

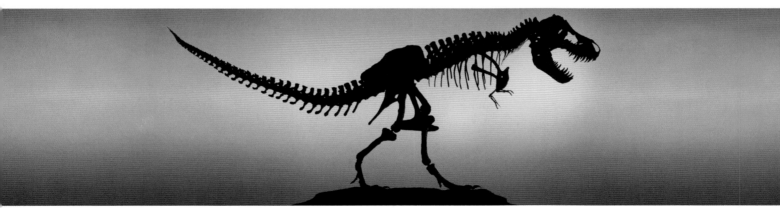

The fossil skeleton of a *Tyrannosaurus rex*, excavated in the Hell Creek Formation of South Dakota, USA

WEBSITES ON LIFE DURING THE MESOZOIC ERA

www.ucmp.berkeley.edu/mammal/mammal.html An introduction to mammals.

https://ucmp.berkeley.edu/cenozoic/cenozoic.php A guide to life over the last 66 million years.

www.bbc.co.uk/nature/life/Mammal/by/rank/all A site that explores the life of mammals.

www.enchantedlearning.com/subjects/mammals/Evolution.shtml All about early mammals.

Glossary

abelisaurid A large theropod, typically from the southern hemisphere.

adaptation The way in which an animal or plant changes over generations to suit a different environment.

ammonite A coiled, shelled sea creature, related to the modern octopus and squid.

anatomy The body parts of an animal – the bones, muscles, sense organs and so on.

ancestor A relative from which an animal is descended.

ankylosaur A plant-eating, armoured dinosaur.

Archosauria The large group of animals that includes dinosaurs, crocodiles, birds and their ancestors.

asteroid A large piece of rock or metal from space that may hit moons or planets such as the Earth.

Aves The Latin name for birds.

belemnite A sea creature with an internal shell, related to the modern cuttlefish.

biostratigraphy The use of fossils to date rocks.

breeding Producing offspring.

camouflage The colour, markings or body shape that helps an animal to blend in with its background.

cannibal An animal that eats another of its own species.

Carboniferous The geological period (359–299 mya) when there were great coal forests, and the early amphibians and reptiles evolved.

Carnian The geological age in the late Triassic (237–227 mya) when the first dinosaur fossils are found.

Cenozoic 66 MYA to present day, after the non-bird dinosaurs.

ceratopsian A plant-eating dinosaur with a horn on its head. Many had neck frills.

cimolestid A small, insect-eating mammal that lived from the Late Cretaceous onwards.

Coelurosauria A group of theropods that gave rise to forms such as tyrannosaurs, dromaeosaurids and modern birds.

compsognathid A group of small, flesh-eating dinosaurs of the Late Jurassic and Early Cretaceous.

confuciusornithid An early fossil bird from China.

conifer A tree with cones, such as a pine or spruce.

continental drift The movement of continents over millions of years.

crest A ridge or line of feathers on the head or down the back.

Cretaceous The geological period from 145–65 mya.

crocodilians Crocodiles, alligators and their ancestors.

cycad A tropical plant with fern-like fronds and large cones.

dicynodont A plant-eating, mammal-like reptile that lived during the Permian and Triassic.

digest To break down food in the body so that it can be absorbed.

Dinosauria The formal name for dinosaurs.

dromaeosaurid A small to mid-sized, flesh-eating dinosaur and a close relative of birds.

ecosystem A self-contained community of plants and animals and their environment, such as a desert.

evolution A gradual process of change in the genetic make-up of a species over generations.

extinction The dying out of a species.

extinction, mass The dying out of very many species over a short period time.

fauna The animals that live together in a particular place.

fibres Tough tissues in plants.

formation Unit of rock of a particular age in a particular place.

fossil The ancient remains, trace or impression of an animal or plant, usually found in rocks.

geology The scientific study of rocks and minerals.

gingko A tree related to the conifer, such as the maidenhair tree of China.

global warming The warming of the air and sea on Earth, causing global climate change.

Gondwana The great prehistoric southern continent made up of what is now Africa, South America, Antarctica, Australia and India.

hadrosaur A plant-eating dinosaur often with a head crest.

herbivore A plant-eater.

ichthyosaur A marine reptile that looked like a shark or dolphin.

iguanodont A plant-eating dinosaur of the Middle Jurassic to Late Cretaceous.

Jurassic The geological period from 200–245 mya.

K-Pg Cretaceous-Paleogene (the K comes from the German for Cretaceous).

Laurasia The great prehistoric northern continent made up of what is now North America, Europe and Asia.

magma Hot, melted rock deep under the Earth's crust.

mammal An animal with hair that produces milk for its young.

Maniraptora The group of theropods that includes birds and their closest dinosaur relatives.

membrane A thin layer of tissue in an animal's body.

Mesozoic The geological era (252– 66 mya) that includes the Triassic, Jurassic and Cretaceous.

migrate To move from one part of the world to another to find food or warm weather, or to produce young.

Miocene The geological epoch from 23–5 mya, when large mammals ruled the Earth.

Norian The geological age of the Late Triassic (215–203 mya) when prosauropod dinosaurs lived.

Ornithischia The major dinosaur group that includes ornithopods,

ceratopsians, ankylosaurs and stegosaurs.

ornithischian Describes a plant-eating dinosaur, a member of the Ornithischia.

ornithomimid An 'ostrich dinosaur', a herbivore with long neck and limbs.

ornithopod A plant-eating dinosaur, typically four-legged.

palaeontologist A scientist who studies fossils.

Palaeocene The span of geological time from 66–56 mya, right after the extinction of the dinosaurs.

Pangaea The supercontinent during the Palaeozoic through to the Middle Mesozoic.

plate tectonics The process deep in the Earth that drives the slow movements of the continents.

plesiosaur A long-necked, marine reptile that swam with broad paddles.

pliosaur A massive-headed, short-necked plesiosaur.

pollination The transfer of male cells to fertilize a female flower.

predator An organism that eats another.

prey An animal that is hunted and eaten by another.

primate A monkey or ape.

prosauropod A group of long-necked sauropod cousins that lived during the Late Triassic and Early Jurassic.

pterosaur A flying reptile that lived throughout the Mesozoic.

reptile A group of animals with scaly or feathered skin, which includes

modern crocodilians, turtles and lizards.

rhynchosaur A Triassic plant-eater with a hooked snout.

Saurischia The major dinosaur group that includes the long-necked sauropodomorphs and the theropods.

sauropod A large, long-necked, plant-eating dinosaur.

sauropodomorphs The prosauropods and sauropods.

scute A thick bony plate found on the back of sea turtles, stegosaurus and so on, usually for defence or fighting.

sediment Mud or sand that may turn into rock – mudstone and sandstone.

seed ferns Ancient plants that had leaves like ferns, but were sometimes as big as trees.

species A group of plants and animals that share characteristics.

specimen A fossil bone or skeleton.

spinosaur A large, flesh-eating dinosaur with a sail-like crest along its back.

stegosaur A plant-eating dinosaur with a row of plates down its back.

stratigraphy A branch of geology: the science of dating rocks.

teleost A typical bony fish, such as a salmon or a goldfish.

terrestrial Living on or in the ground on Earth.

therizinosaur A bizarre, plant-eating theropod, from the Cretaceous, that had long, scythe-like claws.

theropod a group of saurischian dinosaurs that gave rise to modern birds.

titanosaur A giant sauropod, typical of the southern continents.

tree fern A primitive tree group with fern-like leaves.

Triassic The span of geological time from 252–201 mya.

troodontid A slender, flesh-eating dinosaur closely related to birds.

tyrannosaur A large, flesh-eating dinosaur of the Middle Jurassic to Late Cretaceous.

tyrannosaurid A more advanced tyrannosaur group that arose in the Late Cretaceous.

vertebrae The bones that make up the spinal column.

Index

Acknowledgements

The Publisher would like to thank the following for permission to reproduce their material. Every care has been taken to trace copyright holders.

Top = t; Bottom = b; Centre = c; Left = l; Right = r

Pages 10tr, 10br Stocktrek Images Inc/Alamy Stock Photo, 10tr Herschel Hoffmeyer/Shutterstock; 11tr Universidad Federal of Rio do Sul, Brazil; 12lc Grupo Paleo, Argentina; 12lcb Corbis/Diego Goldberg/Sygma, 12lb Corbis/Louie Psihoyos; 13 Corbis/Hubert Stadler; 14bl with the Kind Permission of the Natural History Museum, London; 16tr Corbis/Louie Psihoyos, 16b Millard H. Sharp/Science Photo Library; 17tcr Alamy/Kevin Schafer; 17br Shutterstock/psamtik; 18t warpaint/Shutterstock,18b Bjoern Wylezich/Shutterstock; 19t Gary Hincks/Science Photo Library, 19b Chris Hellier/Science Photo Library; 20 Getty Images/DK; 21tr EvaK, 21cr Jens Lallensack; 22cl Natural History Museum, Stuttgart, 22–23t James Kuether/Science Photo Library, 22br Natural History Museum, Stuttgart; 23tr Natural History Museum, London, 23br with thanks to Dr Mallison and his colleagues; 24b Natural History Museum, London, 24–25 Daniel Eskridge/Shutterstock, 25tr Corbis/Bettman; 27cl, 27cr Mohamad Haghani/ Alamy Stock Photo; 28–29c, 28cr Stocktrek Images Inc./Alamy Stock Photo; 29cr Dinosaur Project/University of Bristol, 29br Dinosaur Project/University of Bristol; 30t, 30br Catmando/Shutterstock, 30bl, 39tr Stocktrek Images Inc/Alamy Stock Photo; 31tr with thanks to Doug Mercer; 31tr Science Photo Library/M-Sat Ltd, 31b Getty Images/Sigurgeir Jonasson/Nordic; 35t Dorling Kindersley/UIG/Science Photo Library, 35b Catmando/Shutterstock; 36tr Rob Gay/Dinodomain.com; 36–37 Shutterstock/Oscity; 37tl Shutterstock/Zack Frank; 37tr US Geological Society; 38tr Alamy/John Cancalosi; 38bl Courtesy of UC Museum of Palaeontology, Berkeley University; 38br Kostyantyn Ivanyshen/Shutterstock; 41 John Elk III/Alamy Stock Photo; 43tc Mark Klinger/Carnegie Museum of Natural History; 43tr Mark Klinger/Carnegie Museum of Natural History; 43cr Institute of Vertebrate Palaeontology and Paleoanthropology, Beijing; 44–45 James Kuether/Science Photo Library, 45br Dave Martill/ University of Portsmouth; 45t Getty Images/Matt Cardy; 46cbi Eugen Thome/Shutterstock, 46crii Kostyantyn Ivanyshen/Shutterstock, 46ctii Daniel Eskridge/Shutterstock; 47tl Natural History Museum, London; 47bc Science Photo Library/Michael Marten; 47br Science Photo Library/Sinclair Stammers; 48t SciePro/Shutterstock, 48–49 Mark P. Witton/Science Photo Library, 49tr Mohamad Haghani/Alamy Stock Photo, 49tr Geological Society, 49br Photo 12/Alamy Stock Photo; 50tr Dept of Geology, Augustana College, 50b Dept of Geology, Augustana College; 52bl Pedro Bernardo/Shutterstock; 53tr Alamy/Steve Bly; 54tl Oixxo/Shutterstock; 55b Domnitsky/Shutterstock, 55bl Cjansuebsri/Shutterstock, 55blii JDCarballo/Shutterstock, 55cl Stocktrek Images Inc/Alamy Stock Photo, 55cli Stocktrek Images Inc/Alamy Stock Photo, 55clii Daniel Eskridge/Shutterstock, 55cri Bee_acg/Shutterstock, 55crii Warpaint/Shutterstock, 55t Orla/Shutterstock; 56–57c Michael Rosskothen/Shutterstock, 56–57 Tororo Reaction/Shuttstock, 56–57 soft_light/Shutterstock, 56–57b Somchai Boonpun/Shutterstock; 57b Natural History Museum, London; 58–59c Jose Antonio Penas/Science Photo Library; 59tr Natural History Museum, London, 59b Friedrich Saurer/ Alamy Stock Photo; 60–61 Catmando/Shutterstock; 62tr With thanks to Roger Vaughan; 62br Corbis/Gaylon Wampler/Sygma; 63tr Science Photo Library/Philippe Plailly/Eurelios; 63bl Science Photo Library/Pascal Geotgheluck; 63br Science Photo Library/Philippe Plailly/Eurelios; 64 Corbis/Jonathan Blair; 66b Dotted Yeti/Shutterstock, 66cl Corbis/Louie Psihoyos; 67 Adam Eastland/Alamy Stock Photo; 68b John Sibbick/Science Photo Library; 69b Valentyna Chukhlyebova/Shutterstock; 70–71 Bikeworldtravel/Shutterstock; 72cl Alamy/North Wind Picture Agency; 72cr&b Corbis/Louie Psihoyos; 73t James Kuether/Science Photo Library, 73cr Shutterstock/Francisco Javier Ballester Calonge, 73bl Historic Collection/Alamy Stock Photo; 74–75 Historic Collection/Alamy Stock Photo; 75b Etemenanki3/WikiCommons; 76–77 Daniel Eskridge/Shutterstock; 77b Sciepro/Science Photo Library, 77tr EvaK; 78l Science Photo Library/Emily Rayfield; 78cr Emily Rayfield; 78br Getty Images/Iconica; 79 Dan Barbatala/Alamy Stock Photo, 79br Corbis/Michael Yamashita; 80–81c Bortonia/Getty Images; 81tr Warpaint/Shutterstock, 81br Elenarts/Shutterstock; 83tl Corbis/Jonathan Blair; 83cr Corbis/Jonathan Blair; 83b Natural History Museum, London; 84tl Jaime Chirlnos/Science Photo Library, 84b dpa picture alliance archive/Alamy Stock Photo; 85 Corbis/Louie Psihoyos; 86l Natural History Museum, London, 86br Michael Rosskothen/Shutterstock; 86–87 Lauren Squire/Shutterstock, 86–87c Warpaint/Shutterstock; 87t and back cover Warpaint/Shutterstock, 87cr and back cover Michael Rosskothen/Shutterstock; 88l Ruth French with the kind permission of Mateus Octavio and the Museu da Lourinha, Portugal; 88bl Mateus Octavio/Museu da Lourinha; 89cl Mateus Octavio/Museu da Lourinha; 89bl Getty Images/AFP; 89br Reuters; 90–91 UnderTheSea/Shutterstock, 90b Sciepro/Getty Images, 90tr Elenarts/Shutterstock; 91tl Sciepro/Getty Images, 91tr Mark P. Witton/Science Photo Library; 92b Stocktrek Images, Inc/Alamy Stock Photo; 93cl Laikayiu; 94tr Natural History Museum, London; 94cl Samwingkit; 94br Finblanco; 95 & 96 Corbis/Louie Psihoyos; 98c John Sibbick/Science Photo Library, 98b Ray Bryant; 99t Natural History Museum, London; 99bl Roy Shepherd at discoveringfossils.co.uk; 99br Natural History Museum, London; 100t Natural History Museum/Science Photo Library, 100c Geological Society; 100bl Catmando/Shutterstock; 102l Science Photo Library/George Bernard; 102–103 Love Lego/Shutterstock; 103br The Natural History Museum/Alamy Stock Photo; 103tr Ray Bryant; 104b Elenarts/Shutterstock; 104–105tc Per Andersen/Alamy Stock Photo; 105tr Herschel Hoffmeyer/Shutterstock 106b Getty/NGS; 107 Professor Mike Benton; 108c David Dilcher and Sun Ge; 110b Stocktrek Images Inc/Alamy Stock Photo; 111t Martin Shields/Alamy Stock Photo, 111c Catmando/Shutterstock; 112l Krys Bailey/Alamy Stock Photo, 112r Sebastian Kaulitzki/Alamy Stock Photo; 113 Brown CM. 2017. An exceptionally preserved armored dinosaur reveals the morphology and allometry of osteoderms and their horny epidermal coverings. PeerJ 5:e4066 https://doi.org/10.7717/peerj.4066; 114l Getty/Spencer Platt; 114–115 Sergey Krasovskiy/Getty Images; 115tr With thanks for Jingmai O'Connor; 116cl Dr Zhiou Zhonge, 116cr Jaime Chirinos/Science Photo Library; 117cr, Natural History Museum, London, 117bl Stocktrek Images Inc/Alamy Stock Photo, 117tl Tiouraren (Y.-C. Tsai)/WikiCommons; 117tr Steve Vidler/Alamy Stock Photo; 118b Catmando/Shutterstock; 119t, National Geographic Image Collection/Alamy Stock Photo, 119c Zoonar GmbH/Alamy Stock Photo, 119b REUTERS/Alamy Stock Photo; 120cl Getty/DK, 120br Valentyna Chukhlyebova/Shutterstock; 120–121 Lou Maher; 121tr Craig Larcom/ Alamy Stock Photo, 121b Courtesy of Yale University; 123tl Valentyna Chukhlyebova/Shutterstock, 123tr Warpaint/Shutterstock, 123b Catmando/Shutterstock; 122–123 Stocktrek Images Inc/Alamy Stock Photo; 124bl Natural History Museum, London; 125 Getty/AFP; 126tr Museum of Victoria, Australia; 127br Geological Society of Australia, Victoria Division; 130cl Getty/Topical Press Agency; 130cr Alamy/Marcus Wilson-Smith; 130b Getty/Hulton; 131tl Christian Masnaghetti/Stocktrek Images, 131cl MShieldsPhotos/Alamy Stock Photo; 131cr Corbis/Louie Psihoyos; 132cl Corbis/Louie Psihoyos; 132–133 Corbis/Louie Psihoyos; 133t Dean Steadman/Kingfisher; 134tl dpa picture alliance archive/Alamy Stock Photo, 134tr Stocktrek Images Inc/Alamy Stock Photo, 134bl Gondwana Studios; 134–135 Mohamad Haghani/Alamy Stock Photo; 135tl Eduard Solà/WikiCommons, 135br Gunnar Reiss, 135tr Stocktrek Images Inc/Alamy Stock Photo; 136–137 Walter Geiersperger/Getty Images; 137tl Evgeniy Mahnyov/Shutterstock, 137bl Mohamad Haghani/Alamy Stock Photo; 138cr Daniel Eskridge/Shutterstock; 139 Natural History Museum, London; 139cr Photoshot; 140l Alamy/Bob Gibbons, 140r Mark P. Witton /Science Photo Library; 141tr Stocktrek Images Inc/Alamy Stock Photo, 141tr Postproduct/Shutterstock; 142cr Walter Myers/Stocktrek Images/Getty Images; 143tl Getty/Tim Boyle, 143br talk|contribs/WikiCommons; 142–143 and back cover Herschel Hoffmeyer/Shutterstock; 144b CookiesForDevo/Shutterstock; 144–145 James Kuether/Science Photo Library; 145br DM7/Shutterstock; 146l Natural History Museum, London; 146cl Andrew Farke and Lukas Panzarin, 146cr James Kuether/Science Photo Library, 146b Ton Bangkeaw/Shutterstock; 147 Mark P. Witton/Science Photo Library; 148r Dorling Kindersley/UIG/Science Photo Library; 149tl Natural History Museum London/Science Photo Library, 149tr James Kuether/Science Photo Library, 149bl Millard H. Sharp/Science Photo Library, 149br Dean Steadman/Kingfisher; 150bl Stilrentfoto/Shutterstock; 154 Corbis/Louie Psihoyos.

The publishers would like to thank the following artists: Julian Baker (104b); Barry Croucher (Art Agency) (136–137); Peter Bull Agency (92c, 92bl, 93tl, 93tr, 93br, 102–10, 110tr, 110b, 111t, 111bl, 111br, 116tr, 116-117, 117tl, 117tr, 117cl); Ben Jones (34, 40l, 40c, 40br); Jane Pritchard/Linden Artists (82l); Roger Stewart (134–135, 135tl, 135tr); Sebastian Quigley (18r, 19tl, 30, 46, 76, 77, 84tl, 88br, 89tr, 98tr, 129, 131t, 131tr, 138l, 138cr, 138br, 139bl, 142cl, 150–151, 150b, 151); Stuart Jackson-Carter (Art Agency) (137cr, 137c, 137br, 137r, 140bl, 140–141, 141tr, 141b); Thomas Bayley (142b, 143tr, 143cr, 143r); all other illustrations by Steve and Sam Weston.